CHARLES DICKENS:

AN INTRODUCTION TO HIS NOVELS

STUDIES IN LANGUAGE AND LITERATURE

CHARLES DICKENS

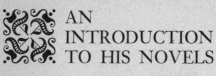

AN
INTRODUCTION
TO HIS NOVELS

E.D.H. JOHNSON

PRINCETON UNIVERSITY

RANDOM HOUSE~NEW YORK

FOR ALEXANDER, GEOFFREY
AND VICTORIA

FOREWORD

The need which this book is intended to fill is indicated by its full title. It has been written for the general reader or the student who does not pretend to specialized knowledge, but who may welcome the background information here provided as a means of enhancing his understanding and enjoyment of a very great novelist.

The first half of the volume is largely factual; the second half critical. Chapters One, Two, and Three attempt to condense what it is important to know about Dickens' life, his age, and his peculiarly intimate relationship with the Victorian reading public. The ensuing chapters trace in broad outline the writer's artistic development. The choice of plot, character, and setting as the topics for critical discussion may seem old-fashioned. Yet, these were the aspects under which Dickens viewed the novel form, both in his own practice and that of others; and most of the best contemporary criticism of his work is referable to one or another of these traditional categories.

Its title may suggest that the present volume duplicates the contents of K. J. Fielding's excellent little study, Charles Dickens: A Critical Introduction *(1958; second edition enlarged, 1965). Professor Fielding, however, follows a chronological plan, examining each of Dickens' novels in turn.*

I am greatly indebted to the counsel of my friend and former student, Professor Robert L. Patten, Department of English, Byrn Mawr College.

E.D.H.J.
PRINCETON, NEW JERSEY
January 1968

CONTENTS

CHARLES DICKENS:

AN INTRODUCTION TO HIS NOVELS

ONE
PROFESSIONAL CAREER

I begin to doubt whether I had anything to do with a book called "Dombey," or ever sat over number five (not finished a fortnight yet) day after day, until I half began . . . to think it the only reality in life, and to mistake all the realities for shortlived shadows.

LETTER FROM CHARLES DICKENS
TO THE COUNTESS OF BLESSINGTON
—JANUARY 24, 1847

You know my life . . . , and my character, and what has had its part in making them successful; and the more you see of me, the better perhaps you may understand that the intense pursuit of any idea that takes complete possession of me, is one of the qualities that makes me different—sometimes for good; sometimes I dare say for evil—from other men.

LETTER FROM CHARLES DICKENS
TO HIS WIFE
—DECEMBER 5, 1853

I hold my inventive capacity on the stern condition that it must master my whole life, often have complete possession of me, make its own demands upon me, and sometimes for months together put everything else

away from me. If I had not   LETTER FROM CHARLES DICKENS
known long ago that my   TO MRS. WINTER
place could never be held   —APRIL 3, 1855
unless I were at any
moment ready to devote myself to it entirely, I should have
dropped out of it very soon. . . . Whoever is devoted to
an Art must be content to deliver himself wholly up to it,
and to find his recompense in it.

SKED ABOUT HIS FAMOUS SON'S EDUCATION, JOHN DICKENS IS REPORTED TO HAVE MADE THE JOCOSE REPLY, "WHY, INDEED, SIR—HA! HA!—HE MAY BE SAID TO have educated himself." To the virtual truth of this statement Charles Dickens' early life bears witness. From 1817 to 1822, between his fifth and tenth years, he lived at Chatham on the southeastern coast of England, where his father was employed as pay clerk in the naval dockyard. Although the boy received some rudimentary instruction in English and even Latin from his mother and for a time attended a dame school similar to that portrayed in the opening pages of *Great Expectations*, it was not until the end of this period that he enjoyed an all too brief exposure to solid instruction under an excellent and sympathetic master, named William Giles. Before this, however, Dickens' imagination had been aroused to precocious activity by less orthodox influences. In an autobiographical essay, entitled "Nurses' Stories," he recounts how he was introduced as a child to the realms of fairy and folklore through the hair-raising bedtime yarns of his nursemaid, who lives on as Peggotty in *David Copperfield*. Before long Dickens discovered his father's library, made up of cheap reprints of the great standard works of fiction. The delight which attended their perusal is vividly recorded in the following passage of David Copperfield's youthful recollections:

My father had left a small collection of books in a little room up-stairs, to which I had access (for it adjoined my own) and which nobody else in our house ever troubled. From that blessed little room, Roderick Random, Peregrine Pickle, Humphrey Clinker, Tom Jones, the Vicar of Wakefield, Don Quixote, Gil Blas, and Robinson Crusoe, came out, a glorious host, to keep me company. They kept alive my fancy, and my hope of something beyond that place and time,—they, and the Arabian Nights, and the Tales of the Genii, . . . I have been Tom Jones (a child's Tom Jones, a harmless creature) for a week together. I have sustained my own idea of Roderick Random for a month at a stretch, I verily believe. . . .

This was my only and my constant comfort. When I think of it, the picture always rises in my mind, of a summer evening, the boys at play in the churchyard, and I sitting on my bed, reading as if for life. Every barn in the neighbourhood, every stone in the church, and every foot of the churchyard, had some association of its own, in my mind, connected with these books, and stood for some locality made famous in them. I have seen Tom Pipes go climbing up the church-steeple; I have watched Strap, with the knapsack on his back, stopping to rest himself upon the wicket-gate; and I *know* that Commodore Trunnion held that club with Mr. Pickle, in the parlour of our little village alehouse.

According to John Forster, the novelist's biographer, the *Tales of the Genii* inspired Dickens' earliest writings, including "a tragedy called *Misnar*, the Sultan of India." From this time also dates an enduring fascination with all varieties of public entertainments. The boy was taken to the theatre and to pantomimes in London and Rochester, and in emulation of these shows achieved a local reputation as an impromptu performer. Forster states that: "He told a story offhand so well, and sang small comic songs so especially well, that he used to be elevated on chairs and tables, both at home and abroad for more effective display of these talents. . . ."

For the rest, a lad as observant and alert to new impressions as the young Dickens found opportunity enough for his sense of adventure in the region about Chatham and Rochester, so rich in historical associations and surviving traditions. "All my early readings and early imaginations dated from this place," he wrote in after years; and the nostalgic tone of many of the pieces in *The Uncommercial Traveller* testifies that the writer, like Wordsworth, continued to derive consolation from recalling this "fair seedtime" of his soul. Indeed, in periods of crisis Dickens was wont to make pilgrimages back to the scenes of his early life, until in 1857 he purchased as his final home Gad's Hill, the country house which he had first seen and admired in the Chatham days and which his father had promised that he might someday own if he worked hard enough. This part of England came to stand for what he thought of as the Eden of childhood innocence; and the poignancy with which he mourned its loss pervades the atmosphere of the passages in *Pickwick Papers*, *David Copperfield*, *Great Expectations*, and *The Mystery of Edwin Drood*, which are set in the locality.

Overnight the youthful idyll came to an end. John Dickens was transferred to London, and with this move his fortunes began to decline. He was a clever, but improvident man, more attentive to the affairs of others than to his own, like Micawber of whom he was partly the original. The family took up residence in Camden Town, the poorest of the London suburbs. Soon it was necessary to sell off household effects, Dickens' cherished books being the first things to go. Unable to meet his financial obligations, the father sought refuge

in Marshalsea Prison under the provisions of the In-
solvent Debtors' Act, and he was joined there by his
wife and younger children.

Charles, the oldest son, was left to shift for himself. Through a family connection he went to work in
Warren's Blacking Warehouse in the Strand, where for
six shillings a week he was set the task of pasting labels
on bottles. Although he subsequently looked back on
this vassalage as of interminable duration, it lasted not
much longer than three months. His duties, quickly
mastered, were not unduly taxing; and he was well
enough treated by his rough associates, who respected
the gentlemanly pretensions which he had acquired
from his father. Nevertheless, the menial nature of his
duties left the sensitive boy with a feeling of having
been degraded. More desolating still was the extinction
of further hope for the education which he so pas-
sionately desired and to which he felt that he was entitled. But deeper than either of these humiliations lay
the despairing conviction that he had been unjustly and
wantonly abandoned, consigned to the company of
homeless waifs who roamed the London streets.

For many years afterwards Dickens could not bring
himself to assess the scars left by this ordeal. So
resolutely did he hide them that his family only learned
the facts from Forster's *Life* after the novelist was dead.
Indeed, they might never have been known if, nearly a
quarter of a century later in 1847, Forster had not
heard a friend of John Dickens remark that he remembered having seen the boy at his place of employment.
Forster's curiosity over this chance discovery moved
Dickens to write the fragment of an autobiography
which he subsequently entrusted to his friend when he
decided to incorporate the substance of his recollections almost verbatim in the Murdstone and Grinby
episode of *David Copperfield*.

As given in full in Forster's *Life*, the original account movingly depicts the feelings of outrage and bitter resentment left by this youthful experience. "It is wonderful to me," he writes,

how I could have been so easily cast away at such an age. It is wonderful to me, that, even after my descent into the poor little drudge I had been since we came to London, no one had compassion enough on me—a child of singular abilities, quick, eager, delicate, and soon hurt, bodily or mentally—to suggest that something might have been spared, as certainly it might have been, to place me at any common school. Our friends, I take it, were tired out. No one made any sign. My father and mother were quite satisfied. They could hardly have been more so, if I had been twenty years of age, distinguished at a grammar-school, and going to Cambridge.

And he continues, after describing his fellow workers:

No words can express the secret agony of my soul as I sunk into this companionship; compared these every day associates with those of my happier childhood; and felt my early hopes of growing up to be a learned and distinguished man, crushed in my breast. The deep remembrance of the sense I had of being utterly neglected and hopeless; of the shame I felt in my position; of the misery it was to my young heart to believe that, day by day, what I had learned, and thought, and delighted in, and raised my fancy and my emulation up by, was passing away from me, never to be brought back any more; cannot be written. My whole nature was so penetrated with the grief and humiliation of such considerations, that even now, famous and caressed and happy, I often forget in my dreams that I have a dear wife and children; and wander desolately back to that time of my life.

After John Dickens, who had received a timely legacy, emerged from the Marshalsea, he arranged in turn for Charles' release from the blacking warehouse,

although Mrs. Dickens would have been content to
have her son remain there. The novelist never forgave
his parents for their treatment. Some of the father's
traits are embodied in William Dorrit, as well as
Micawber, while Mrs. Nickleby and Mrs. Micawber
were modeled in part on the mother. More revealing,
however, is the theme of parental neglect prominent
in virtually all of the novels. Most of their protagonists
are orphans or half-orphans, harbored in the homes of
surrogate parents. The sense of insecurity instilled by
this period of abandonment was to have its lifelong
aftermath in other ways. It is reflected in Dickens'
determination never again to be at the mercy of circumstance, and in the ruthlessness which as a result
characterized all his business dealings. And this concern with material well-being in turn dominates his
writings. As Humphry House has written:

Money is a main theme of nearly every book that Dickens
wrote: getting, keeping, spending, owing, bequeathing
provide the intricacies of his plots; character after character is constructed round an attitude to money. Social
status without it is subordinate.

On the credit side must be reckoned certain im-
ponderable gains traceable to this period when the
young Dickens was thrown entirely on his own resources. For want of other diversion, he formed the
habit of wandering the city streets, and as an onlooker
at the "magic lantern" of the thronged metropolis,
began to discipline his phenomenally accurate and re-
tentive powers of observation. In the process he acquired the kind of knowledge which Mr. Weller
prided himself on having provided for Sam: "I took a
good deal o' pains with his eddication, sir: let him run
in the streets when he was wery young, and shift for
his-self. It's the only way to make a boy sharp, sir."

Dickens' formal schooling came to an end with two years at Wellington House Academy, the brutal headmaster of which became Mr. Creakle in *David Copperfield*. At this establishment, where he was remembered as a waggish and somewhat dandified boy of quick parts, his literary and theatrical interests revived. When he was fifteen, he left to become office boy in a law firm, and soon after began to teach himself shorthand. On the basis of this skill (the arduous mastery of which is so hilariously described in *David Copperfield*), he was promoted in his seventeenth year to the position of legal reporter in Doctors' Commons.

Henceforth his progress was rapid. He reported parliamentary proceedings for a succession of newspapers, until at the age of twenty-two he took over this function for the influential *Morning Chronicle*. In tribute to the proficiency with which he carried out his exacting duties, an editor declared that among the eighty or ninety reporters in the gallery Dickens "occupied the very highest rank not merely for accuracy in reporting, but for marvelous quickness of transcript." Dickens filled the intervals when Parliament was in recess by traveling about England to cover political campaigns like that at Eatanswill in *Pickwick Papers*, and in this way extended his knowledge of the contemporary scene beyond the limits of London. He delighted in the rough-and-ready scramble of a journalist's life. "I have pursued the calling of a reporter," he told a gathering of newspapermen thirty years later,

under circumstances of which many of my brethren at home in England here, many of my modern successors, can form no adequate conception. I have often transcribed for the printer from my shorthand notes, important public speeches in which the strictest accuracy was required, and a mistake in which would have been to a young man severely compromising, writing on the palm of my hand, by the light of a dark lantern, in a post chaise and four, galloping through a wild country, all through the dead of night, at the then surprising rate of fifteen miles an hour. . . . I have worn my knees by writing on them on the backrow of the old gallery of the old House of Commons; and I have worn my feet by standing to write in a preposterous pen in the House of Lords, where we used to be huddled together like so many sheep, kept in waiting, say, until the woolsack might want re-stuffing. I have been, in my time, belated on miry by-roads, towards the small hours, in a wheelless carriage, with exhausted horses and drunken postboys, and have got back in time for publication. . . .

It was in London, however, that Dickens always felt most at home; and during these years he continued to deepen that intimacy with every aspect of its manifold life which qualified him to be the first great English novelist of the modern city. An acquaintance said: "I thought I knew something of the town; but after a little talk with Dickens I found I knew nothing. He knew it all from Bow to Brentford. . . . He could imitate in a manner I never saw equalled the low population of the streets of London in all their varieties." The emergent lower middle class was awaiting its historian; and when Dickens first turned to imaginative writing, this was the segment of the populace which especially attracted his attention. His first original piece, entitled "A Dinner at Poplar Walk" (later renamed "Mr. Minns and His Cousin") appeared in the *Monthly Magazine* in December 1833. A succession of sketches and tales, eventually numbering fifty-nine, were published in the *Morning Chronicle* and its offshoot the *Evening Chronicle*, as well as in the *Monthly Magazine* and *Bell's Life in London*. For this work the author adopted in August 1834 the pseudonym of "Boz," a corruption of Moses, the pet name of a younger brother. Dickens' literary career was fully launched when the publisher, John Macrone, contracted for a collection of these sketches, which came out in two volumes, illustrated by George Cruikshank, on the writer's twenty-fourth birthday. The contents were fittingly described by the full title: *Sketches by Boz: Illustrative of Everyday Life and Everyday People*. A Second Series was published in 1837. Of Dickens' achievement in this initial venture, Forster wrote:

it is a book that might have stood its ground, even if it had stood alone, as containing unusually truthful observation of a sort of life between the middle class and the low, which, having few attractions for bookish observers, was quite unhacknied ground. It had otherwise also the very special merit of being in no respect bookish or commonplace in its descriptions of the old city with which its writer was so familiar. It was a picture of every-day London at its best and worst, in its humours and enjoyments as well as its sufferings and sins, pervaded everywhere not only with the absolute reality of the things depicted, but also with that subtle sense and mastery of feeling which gives to the reader's sympathies invariably right direction, and awakens consideration, tenderness, and kindness precisely for those who most need such help.

Dickens' literary and repertorial activities by no means expended his boundless energy. At this period he attended the theater almost nightly, and took part in amateur dramatics whenever the opportunity offered. Indeed, he seriously considered becoming an actor, and to prepare himself, spent long hours in memorizing and rehearsing roles. Although from time to time he tried his hand at writing skits in the popular contemporary modes, he was most attracted by the dramatic projection of character. By preference he sought out plays which exhibited the talents of the leading players of the day, among whom his favorite was the great master of pantomime, Charles Mathews. In estimating his own qualifications, he wrote: "I believed I had a strong perception of character and oddity, and a natural power of reproducing in my own person what I observed in others."

These also were the years in which Dickens survived a second emotional crisis, so damaging to his self-esteem that he omitted all reference to it in his fragment of an autobiography. At seventeen he met and fell deliriously in love with Maria Beadnell, the daughter of a bank official. Although disparity in social position, as well as the girl's flighty nature, portended disappointment from the outset, Dickens' infatuation dragged indecisively on through four years before her father put an end to the relationship in May 1833. Recalling the raptures and misery which Maria occasioned him, Dickens wrote more than twenty years later when she reopened correspondence:

I have always believed since, and always shall to the last, that there never was such a faithful and devoted poor fellow as I was. Whatever of fancy, romance, energy, passion, aspiration and determination belong to me, I never have separated and never shall separate from the hard-hearted little woman—you—whom it is nothing to say I would have died for, with the greatest alacrity! I never can think, and I never seem to observe, that other young people are in such desperate earnest or set so much, so long, upon one absorbing thought. It is a matter of perfect certainty to me that I began to fight my way out of poverty and obscurity, with one perpetual idea of you. . . . I have never been so good a man since, as I was when you made me wretchedly happy. I shall never be half so good a fellow any more.

This experience of first love survives in David Copperfield's courtship of Dora Spenlow, which is an instructive example of how the material of real life undergoes artistic transmutation. Just as the novelist provides for his hero at Dr. Strong's Academy the kind of educational opportunity of which he had been deprived, and just as David becomes an articled clerk in Doctors' Commons where his creator had been a humble reporter, so Dickens allows his *alter ego* to try the not unmixed joys of wedded life with Maria's counterpart before she is removed from the scene in the interests of David's further development. In the aftermath Dickens took a crueller revenge for his twice-frustrated hopes. Recognizing her portrait in Dora, Maria, now long married, made overtures in 1855, to which Dickens, who had become increasingly unhappy in his own domestic life, at first eagerly responded, only to find that the pretty and vivacious girl whom he remembered had become a rather dumpy and gushing middle-aged woman. When she appeared again in his fiction, it was as one of his great comic conceptions, the ineffably foolish Flora Finching of *Little Dorrit*.

The year 1836 was Dickens' *annus mirabilis*. In April he married Catherine Hogarth, the daughter of the editor of the *Evening Chronicle*, who was to bear him ten children. At the end of the previous month the *Times* had announced as forthcoming the first monthly installment of a new work by "Boz," entitled *The Posthumous Papers of the Pickwick Club*. The success of the *Sketches* had led the newly established publishing house of Chapman and Hall to invite the author to compose the prose commentary for a sequence of sporting plates by the popular artist Robert Seymour. Dickens accepted the offer with the stipulation that the subject matter be broadened in scope and that he be given a larger share in determining it. When Seymour committed suicide before the publication of the second

number, Dickens assumed full control. The monthly
text was considerably expanded to thirty-two pages
and the number of illustrations (no longer regarded
as the *raison d'être* of the work) was reduced from
three or four to two. Dickens chose as Seymour's suc-
cessor Hablot K. Browne, "Phiz," who so scrupulously
carried out the writer's suggestions for the cuts that
he was to be the principal illustrator of the novels for
many years to come. From the outset it was decided
that *Pickwick Papers* should appear in twenty parts
over a period of nineteen months (the last issue being a
double one). The undertaking did not get off to an
especially auspicious start; only four hundred copies
of the first number were printed for distribution on
March 31. With the fourth number in which Sam
Weller made his entrance, however, sales rapidly
climbed until they reached the unprecedented figure of
forty thousand. At twenty-five Dickens found himself
the most widely read author in England.

In the first flush of popularity Dickens recklessly
accepted new commitments, and in so doing ran the
danger of overextending himself, while he laid the
basis for future disputes with a succession of publishers,
whom he habitually treated in a somewhat cavalier
manner. In May 1836 he contracted with Macrone for
a three-volume novel, to be entitled *Gabriel Vardon,
The Locksmith of London.* The rights for this work,
renamed *Barnaby Rudge*, were later acquired by
Richard Bentley, from whom they passed to Chapman
and Hall, who finally brought it out in monthly parts
more than four years later. Meanwhile, Dickens had
taken on the editorship of *Bentley's Miscellany* in
which *Oliver Twist* began to appear in February 1837,
when the parts of *Pickwick Papers* had run only half
their course. In 1837 Dickens also edited for Bentley
the *Memoirs of Grimaldi*, the famous clown. On con-

cluding *Pickwick Papers* in November 1837, but while *Oliver Twist* was still half finished, Dickens agreed to write for Chapman and Hall another novel in twenty parts. This was *Nicholas Nickleby*, begun in February 1838 after the author had paid a visit to Yorkshire to inspect the notorious school on which Dotheboys Hall was modeled.

In the midst of these hectic literary activities Dickens was afflicted by a third blow, which, like his servitude in the blacking warehouse and his infatuation for Maria Beadnell, shadowed his future career. At the time of their marriage, Catherine Dickens' younger sister, Mary, aged sixteen, had become a member of the household. A year later in May 1837 she died with an "awful suddenness" in Dickens' arms. She was a sweet-natured girl of exceptional promise, and had won her brother-in-law's deep devotion. Shattered by grief, he was, for the first and only time in his career, unable to meet the deadlines for the installments of the two stories which he then had in progress. Throughout life he wore the ring which he had slipped from the dying girl's finger. For many months she appeared to him nightly in dreams, and he long cherished the hope of being buried at her side. It seems certain that her early death became associated in Dickens' imagination with his own unfulfilled youth. Some of her qualities were embodied in the character of Rose Maylie in *Oliver Twist*, and she inspired Little Nell. Indeed, all of Dickens' saintly girl heroines owe something to his sorrowful memories of this brief, but strangely intense relationship.

Before the termination of *Oliver Twist*, Dickens relinquished the editorship of *Bentley's Miscellany* and began negotiations which resulted in the consolidation of all of his literary affairs in the hands of Chapman and Hall. The essayists, Addison, Steele, and especially

Goldsmith, had helped form the novelist's manner; and he now projected a weekly magazine which would reproduce the range of topics, as well as the colloquial tone, of the eighteenth-century periodicals. *Master Humphrey's Clock*, as it was named, first appeared in March 1840, with an initial circulation of seventy thousand. What the public wanted from the editor, however, was a new novel rather than a mixed bag of odds and ends, the by-products of his teeming fancy; and when sales began to decline, Dickens decided to abandon his original plan and to convert the publication exclusively into a vehicle for his fiction. From the fourth number, therefore, each issue was largely devoted to *The Old Curiosity Shop*, "the little child-story" which had been originally designed as a short tale. Although the Preface to *Master Humphrey's Clock* expressed the hope that "to shorten the intervals of communication between himself and his readers would be to bind more closely [their] pleasant relations," he found both now and later the limitations of weekly serialization severely cramping, in contrast to the ampler scope provided by his preferred method of publication in monthly parts. Nevertheless, the sales of *Master Humphrey's Clock* climbed to one hundred thousand while *The Old Curiosity Shop* was running; and the same form was retained for the immediately succeeding story, *Barnaby Rudge*, the historical novel of the Gordon Riots of 1780, which had first been planned over four years earlier.

After *Barnaby Rudge* had run its course in 1841, Dickens discontinued his weekly and turned to preparations for his first visit to the United States, in the winter and spring of 1842. The novelist's American public was as extensive and enthusiastic as his following in Great Britain; and despite his outspoken statements about the need for an international copyright law to prevent the wholesale pirating of works by English writers, he was lionized throughout most of a journey which took him and Mrs. Dickens as far west as St. Louis. Yet, having come over in the eager expectation of finding a nation emancipated from the tyrannous usages of the old world, Dickens soon became disillusioned by his American experiences. He wrote to Forster:

I believe that there is no country, on the face of the earth, where there is less freedom of opinion on any subject in reference to which there is a broad difference of opinion than in this. . . . I do fear the heaviest blow ever dealt at liberty will be dealt by this country, in the failure of its example to the earth.

Indignation over the coarse manners of the Americans and over such evils as the traffic in slaves further darkened Dickens' views; and a letter to the actor Macready reached the bitter conclusion:

This is not the republic I came to see; this is not the republic of my imagination. . . . The more I think of its youth and strength, the poorer and more trifling in a thousand aspects it appears in my eyes. In everything of which it has made a boast—excepting its education of the people and its care for poor children—it sinks immeasurably below the level I had placed it upon; and England, even England, bad and faulty as the old land is, and miserable as millions of her people are, rises in comparison.

By October Dickens had gathered his impressions into *American Notes*, which went through four editions by the end of the year and which, not surprisingly, provoked howls of indignation from his overseas readers. But the last word was still to be said. The first monthly installment of *Martin Chuzzlewit* came out in January 1843. When sales fell below the author's

expectations, he transferred the scene of the protagonist's adventures to America in the fifteenth chapter,
hoping thereby to reinvigorate the interest of at least
the British portion of his audience.*

In a further overt bid for the popular market Dickens in 1843 inaugurated his series of annual Christmas
books. The first of these five novellas was "A Christmas
Carol," followed by "The Chimes" (1844), "The
Cricket in the Hearth" (1845), "The Battle of Life"
(1846), and "The Haunted Man" (1848). As an indication of how deeply the writer could become involved
even in work undertaken primarily for financial gain,
there is his admission to a friend that in writing "A
Christmas Carol" he "wept and laughed, and wept
again, and excited himself in a most extraordinary
manner in the composition; and thinking whereof he
walked about the black streets of London fifteen and
twenty miles many a night when all sober folks had
gone to bed."

The writing of six major novels in seven years had
momentarily drained Dickens' vitality, tremendous
though it was; and in July 1844 he took his family for
a year's holiday in Italy, with headquarters at Genoa.
This sojourn among the pleasure-loving people of
southern Europe was recorded in a volume entitled
Pictures from Italy (1846); but the real profit which
Dickens derived from this vacation was the opportunity
it provided to gain perspective on affairs at home. The
vestiges of outworn traditions surviving on the con-
tinent made him aware as never before of the compul-
sive thrust for change accompanying the industrial
revolution in his own country; and "The Chimes,"

* Forster suggests, however, that the introduction of an American setting was motivated less by Dickens' desire to pump
up sales for his new novel than by "the challenge to make
good" the allegations in *American Notes*.

written in Genoa, exhibits in its treatment of class antagonism a new note of urgency, as well as a profounder awareness of social injustice. Dickens' avowed intent in this story was to strike "a great blow for the poor"; "if my design be anything at all," he asserted, "it has a grip upon the very throat of the time."

On his return to England in 1845 Dickens immersed himself in amateur theatricals with a fervor which suggests that through the make-believe world of the stage he achieved the same imaginative release which accompanied the act of fictional creation. To the novelist Bulwer Lytton he confessed: "Assumption has charms for me—I hardly know for how many wild reasons—so delightful that I feel a loss of, oh! I can't say what exquisite foolery, when I lose a chance of being someone in voice, etc. not at all like myself." He set about forming a company of his literary and artist friends. In addition to acting parts himself, he took on the duties of director, stage manager, scene designer, property man, even prompter. The first production was Jonson's *Every Man in His Humour* with Dickens in the role of Bobadil, but the repertory was soon extended. Not only at this time, but in 1847–1848 and again in 1850–1852, the company, which Dickens had brought to a high degree of professional skill, played before crowded houses, both in London and throughout the provinces. One run of nine performances, given over a period of three months in 1848, grossed more than £2500. The productions were invariably offered as charitable benefits, the last series being in support of the Guild of Literature and Art, which Dickens helped originate to provide for impoverished writers and artists.

In connection with Dickens' dramatic activities, his persistent fondness for shows of all kinds must again be emphasized. His correspondence testifies to the fact that, wherever he chanced to be, he never missed the opportunity to attend a theatrical exhibition, whether it was *Mazeppa* staged by a circus at Ramsgate, the Italian marionettes in the stable of a Roman *palazzo*, or a French medieval mystery play at a country fair at Arras. Typical is the following comment in a letter to Forster of 1842:

At the Isle of Thanet races yesterday I saw—oh! who shall say what an immense amount of character in the way of inconceivable villainy and blackguardism! I even got some new wrinkles in the way of showmen, conjurors, pea-and-thimblers, and trampers generally.*

In the summer of 1846 Dickens again took his family abroad, this time to Switzerland, where he commenced work on *Dombey and Son*. Progress was slow at the start, for his hand was out after two years' respite from novel writing. More than anything else he missed the stimulation of an urban environment. Of "the absence of streets and numbers of figures," he wrote Forster:

I can't express how much I want these. It seems as if they supplied something to my brain, which it cannot bear, when busy, to lose. For a week or a fortnight I can write prodigiously in a retired place (as at Broadstairs), and a day in London sets me up again and starts me. But the toil and labour of writing, day after day, without that magic lantern, is IMMENSE! !

Dombey and Son was continued in Paris and completed in London. Dickens had never before taken such pains over planning a story, and the artistic ad-

* Dickens himself became an accomplished magician and delighted to display feats of legerdemain at the children's entertainments he arranged at his London residence, Tavistock House, during the 1850s.

vance is apparent, both in the thematic focus and in the increased control over the ramifications of the narrative. The sales of the first number, exceeding those of *Martin Chuzzlewit* by over ten thousand, relieved the author from any further need for financial anxiety.

David Copperfield was begun early in 1849, shortly after Dickens visited Yarmouth, the home of the Peggottys. The circumstances of the composition of this novel have already been in part described. Forster had made the proposal that he try first-person narrative (conceivably as a result of the brilliant success of Charlotte Brontë's *Jane Eyre* in the previous year); and Dickens' decision to incorporate passages from his early life in this form led to the discontinuance of the autobiography which he had started. Of his satisfaction with the results the author wrote to his friend: "I really think I have done it ingeniously, and with a very complicated interweaving of truth and fiction." Whether or not, as critics have argued, *David Copperfield* was undertaken as a purgative exercise through which the writer was finally able to come to terms with unhappy experiences in his youth, there can be no doubt that it remained Dickens' favorite among his works. On its completion in October 1850, he announced to Forster, "I seem to be sending some part of myself into the shadowy world"; and the Preface of 1869 repeats this sentiment with the addition: "No one can ever believe this Narrative, in the reading, more than I believed it in the writing."

Ever since the demise of *Master Humphrey's Clock*, Dickens had recurrently considered starting a new weekly; and in 1849, concurrently with the writing of *David Copperfield*, he again took up the idea. The deepening social consciousness, manifest in "The Chimes" and *Dombey and Son*, combined with his

prestige as a leading Victorian man of letters, had led
to increasing participation in contemporary reform
movements. A great admirer of Carlyle, he accepted
the intellectual leadership of that thinker, voiced in
such thundering denunciations of the spirit of the
times as *Chartism* and *Past and Present*. As early as
1835 he had met the great public benefactress, Angela
Burdett Coutts, and during the 1840s he was her principal adviser in a number of charitable enterprises, including a home for reformed prostitutes and projects
for slum clearance. His fascination with the criminal
mentality had also led him to make a special study of
current theory and practice in prison administration,
an interest very much to the fore during his travels in
the United States. In the long list of other causes which
enlisted his support, educational systems and sanitary
measures were prominent.

In his new periodical Dickens proposed to canvass
all such issues as they affected the public welfare; but
besides giving vent to his reforming zeal, it was also
to provide the kind of racy coverage of topics of
general interest that characterizes modern news maga-
zines. Forster has well described the resulting editorial
policy:

It was to be a weekly miscellany of general literature; and
its stated objects were to be, to contribute to the enter-
tainment and instruction of all classes of readers, and to
help in the discussion of the more important social questions of the time. It was to comprise short stories by others
as well as himself; matters of passing interest in the live-
liest form that could be given to them; subjects suggested
by books that might most be attracting attention; and
poetry in every number if possible, but in any case something of romantic fancy. This was to be a cardinal point.
There was to be no mere utilitarian spirit; with all familiar things, but especially those repellent on the surface,
something was to be connected that should be fanciful or

kindly; and the hardest workers were to be taught that their lot is not necessarily excluded from the sympathies and graces of imagination.

Household Words, as the weekly was named after long deliberation, made its first appearance on March 30, 1850. With the able assistance of his subeditor, William Henry Wills, Dickens exercised the same autocratic control over its production that he exhibited in the direction of amateur theatricals. He solicited contributions from the principal literary figures of the day, himself read all work submitted, and rigorously edited or gave stringent instructions for the rewriting of pieces which he deemed acceptable. At the same time, out of his vast experience of Victorian reading tastes, he generously helped unfledged writers to get a start. His success in running *Household Words* led Lord Northcliffe, founder of the *Daily Mail* and later owner of the *Times*, to call Dickens the greatest of all magazine editors.

For the serious student of Dickens *Household Words* is an important primary source, not only because the articles reflect the novelist's expanding intellectual horizon, but because many of them present in embryonic form themes which were to be developed in the later work. This is particularly true for the great, so-called "dark" novels of social criticism which now began to appear. The first was *Bleak House*, published in monthly parts from March 1852, and enjoying a steady circulation of nearly thirty-five thousand. Next came *Hard Times*, dedicated to Carlyle and first issued as a weekly serial in *Household Words*, the circulation of which it more than doubled. *Little Dorrit*, again written in monthly numbers, began to appear in December 1855.

During a number of years another serious crisis

in the novelist's private life had been coming on. Despite their large family, husband and wife had never been really compatible since the early days of their union. Catherine Dickens was a well-meaning but ineffectual woman, devoid alike of the social graces and the mental alertness which might have qualified her to take an active part in Charles' public life. To his growing restiveness under the domestic yoke may perhaps be attributed the prevalence of unhappy marriages in *Dombey and Son* and the succeeding novels; and his correspondence increasingly hints at the want of harmony in his home. A letter of 1852 to Mary Boyle, who acted in his dramatic company, sounds a note recurrent in *David Copperfield:* "This is one of what I call my wandering days, before I fall to work. I seem to be always looking at such times for something I have not found in life, but may possibly come to a few thousands of years hence, in some other part of some other system. God knows." And again to Forster three years later Dickens writes: "Why is it, that as with poor David, a sense comes always crushing on me now, when I fall into low spirits, as of one happiness I have missed in life, and one friend and companion I have never made?"

The open break with his wife may be dated from the presentation in 1857 of Wilkie Collins' *The Frozen Deep*, a melodrama in which Dickens played a part anticipatory of Sydney Carton's role in *A Tale of Two Cities*. For the feminine characters he had chosen the well-known actress, Mrs. Ternan, and her two daughters. With the younger of these, Ellen Lawless Ternan, a pretty blonde girl, Dickens became infatuated. Although he conducted the ensuing relationship with such discretion that Ellen remains a shadowy figure in the background, it is now known that their liaison lasted to the end of Dickens' life. The girl's name certainly influenced the naming of the heroines of the last three novels, Estella in *Great Expectations*, Bella Wilfer in *Our Mutual Friend*, and Helena Landless in *The Mystery of Edwin Drood*. The wilful and imperious ways of the first two of these characters represent a noteworthy departure from the earlier ideal of saintly meekness embodied in Florence Dombey, Agnes Wickfield, Esther Summerson, and Amy Dorrit. And there can be no mistaking that Dickens' later fiction explores sexual passion with an intensity and perceptiveness not previously apparent.

In 1858 Dickens permanently separated from Catherine, for whom he maintained a separate establishment, while the majority of their children lived with him at Gad's Hill. To this recently purchased home he was also accompanied by his sister-in-law, Georgina Hogarth, who acted as his housekeeper. She had lived with the Dickens ever since their return from America, and her unfaltering loyalty to the novelist through all the trials of his final years went far to compensate for the still lamented death of Mary Hogarth.

It was during this period that Dickens, against the advice of such intimates as Forster, entered on the first series of paid readings from his works. He doubtless welcomed these performances as a distraction from his domestic difficulties, and there was the added motive of financial gain. The principal inducement, however, was to draw still tighter the ties which united him with his audience by exploiting the dramatic properties of his writings. To Forster he wrote: "Will you then try to think of this reading project (as I do) apart from all personal likings and dislikings, and solely with a view to its effect on that particular relation (personally affectionate and like no other man's) which subsists between me and the public?" The extent to which Dickens had become dependent

on the suffrage of his readers is indicated by the fact
that on June 12, 1858, he had printed on the front
page of *Household Words* a statement reporting that
he and Mrs. Dickens had agreed to separate and de-
nouncing all scandal mongers who might reflect discredit on the reasons for this decision.

Dickens had long been in the habit of trying out
the effect of his works through oral presentation, first
to an inner circle of friends and later in unpaid public
recitations, the first of which was given in December
1853 before the newly founded Birmingham and Midland Institute. He began to read for his own profit on
April 29, 1858, and between that date and October
27, 1859, appeared 125 times before packed auditori-
ums that often accommodated between two and three
thousand. The success of his initial tour was duplicated
on three succeeding occasions, in 1861–1863, in 1866–
1867 (when the novelist made his second trip to the
United States), and in 1868–1870. In all, Dickens gave
423 readings.

The most popular of the passages adapted for delivery included at the outset "A Christmas Carol," the
trial scene from *Pickwick Papers*, Paul Dombey's
death, and Mrs. Gamp. For the second tour the Steer-
forth-Emily episode from *David Copperfield* and
Dotheboys Hall from *Nicholas Nickleby* were added
to a repertoire that eventually included sixteen readings. These appearances enlisted the full range of
Dickens' histrionic talents, and he spared no effort to
refine them. Even though the physical effort of projecting himself night after night into such a variety of
roles began after the first series seriously to under-
mine his health, he became, like one addicted to drugs,
increasingly reliant on the excitement of evoking the
illusory world he shared with his auditors. "So real are
my fictions to myself," he wrote, "that, after hundreds

of nights, I come with a feeling of perfect freshness to that little red table, and laugh and cry with my hearers, as if I had never stood there before."

In 1844 Chapman and Hall had been supplanted by Bradbury and Evans as Dickens' publishers. Falling out with this house, which disliked the publicity attending the separation, he decided in 1859 to return to Chapman and Hall. One result of this change was that Dickens severed connections with *Household Words* and established a new weekly, named *All the Year Round*, which principally differed from its predecessor in that the opening pages of each issue were devoted to the serial publication of extended works of fiction. The initial installment of Dickens' second historical novel, *A Tale of Two Cities*, appearing in the first number, at once established the popularity of *All the Year Round*, which eventually attained a circulation of three hundred thousand. To its pages the novelist also contributed the essays gathered under the title, *The Uncommercial Traveller*, and, starting in December 1860, *Great Expectations*. This story, originally planned in twenty parts, was recast as a weekly serial to take the place of a novel by another author which had adversely affected sales.

Dickens' last completed novel in his preferred form of monthly parts was *Our Mutual Friend*, published between May 1864 and November 1865. The literary activities of these years also included a number of short stories; and although he was never at home within the limitations of this form, these tales present some interesting technical experiments, indicative of the author's readiness to explore new modes of expression. The market for his writings is attested by the fact that he received £1,000 each from American publishers for first rights to "George Silverman's Explanation" and "A Holiday Romance."

During 1863–1864 the first intimations that Dickens was dangerously overtaxing his stamina came with the painful lameness in his left foot which was to torment him through the years remaining. Furthermore, in 1865 he sustained a disabling nervous shock when he and Ellen Ternan nearly lost their lives in a railway accident at Staplehurst. The third reading tour, which took him overseas from December 1867 to April 1868, implanted more favorable impressions of life in the United States than he had brought back from his first visit, although he had constantly to struggle against ill health in meeting his engagements. From these seventy-six readings alone he realized about £20,000.

In preparation for what was to be his farewell series of appearances in England, begun in October 1868, Dickens worked up a version of Sikes' murder of Nancy from *Oliver Twist*, the brutal ferocity of which so exhausted him that it was soon necessary to keep a doctor in attendance. A physical breakdown necessitated the interruption of these performances in April 1869, but Dickens compulsively insisted on resuming them in January and February of the following year. The last reading took place on March 15, less than three months before his death.

Meanwhile, Dickens had in the autumn of 1869 embarked on *The Mystery of Edwin Drood*, a novel which in both subject and method struck out in new directions. It was to be published at monthly intervals in twelve parts. Only six had been completed when on June 8, 1870, after a long day's writing in his chalet on the grounds of Gad's Hill, he suffered the stroke from which he died on the following day. With professional reticence he took to the grave the secret of Drood's murder.

TWO
SOCIAL
BACKGROUND

"*Them Confugion steamers,*" *said Mrs. Gamp, shaking her umbrella again,* "*has done more to throw us out of our reg'lar work and bring ewents on at times when nobody counted on 'em (especially them screeching railroad ones), than all the other frights that ever was took. I have heerd of one young man, a guard upon a railway, only three years opened—well does Mrs. Harris know him, which indeed he is her own relation by her sister's marriage with a master sawyer—as is godfather at this present time to six-and-twenty blessed little strangers, equally unexpected, and all on 'um named after the Ingeins as was the cause. Ugh!*" *said Mrs. Gamp, resuming her apostrophe,* "*one might easy know you was a man's invention, from your disregardlessness of the weakness of our naturs, so one might, you brute!*"

Martin Chuzzlewit,
CHAPTER 40

"*Oh, you're a broth of a boy, ain't you?*" *returned Miss Mowcher, shaking her head violently.* "*I said, what a set of humbugs we were in general, and I showed you the scraps of the Prince's nails to prove it. The Prince's nails do more for me in private families of the genteel sort than all my talents put together. I always carry 'em about; they're the best introduction. If Miss Mowcher cuts the Prince's nails, she must be all right. I give 'em away to the young ladies. They put 'em in albums,*

David Copperfield,
CHAPTER 22

*I believe. Ha! ha! ha! Upon my life, 'the whole social
system' (as the men call it when they make speeches
in Parliament) is a system of Prince's nails!"*

*It does not seem to me to be enough to say of any
description that it is the exact truth. The exact truth
must be there; but the merit or art in the narrator, is the
manner of stating the truth. As to which thing in literature,
it always seems to me that
there is a world to be done.* CHARLES DICKENS, QUOTED BY
And in these times, when JOHN FORSTER, *The Life*
the tendency is to be *of Charles Dickens,* BOOK NINE,
frightfully literal and CHAPTER I
catalogue-like—to make the
*thing, in short, a sort of sum in reduction that any
miserable creature can do in that way—I have an idea
(really founded on the love of what I profess), that the
very holding of popular literature through a kind of popular
dark age, may depend on such fanciful treatment.*

AS HIS EVENTFUL CAREER BEARS WITNESS, DICKENS WAS VERY MUCH A MAN OF HIS TIMES; AND IT IS IN THE FULL CONTEXT OF AN AGE PRIMARILY CHARACTERIZED by rapid change that his writings must, in the first instance, be read if they are to yield their full meaning. Equally partial and therefore reductive are the views of Chesterton and the Pickwickians, who find the best of Dickens in the overflowing vitality of the early novels with their nostalgic looking back to an older order, and the views of writers like Gissing and Shaw, who prefer the later works for their somberly realistic portrayal of the new industrial society. The very grounds for disagreement between the two approaches suggest the importance of establishing a firm historical basis for the criticism of Dickens' achievement.

In their exuberant and heterogeneous inclusiveness, *Pickwick Papers*, *Nicholas Nickleby*, *The Old Curiosity Shop*, and *Martin Chuzzlewit* are unmistakably the work of the same inspired reporter who wrote *Sketches by Boz*. Dickens might have been offering his own apology for these early literary excursions when he had Pickwick say at the end of his pilgrimage:

I shall never regret having devoted the greater part of two years to mixing with different varieties and shades of human character: frivolous as my pursuit of novelty may have appeared to many. . . . If I have done but little good, I trust I have done less harm, and that none of my adventures will be other than a source of amusing and pleasant recollection. . . .

The guise in which The Uncommercial Traveller came before the public in 1860 shows that late in his career the writer still held to the aims with which he had set out:

Figuratively speaking, I travel for the great house of Human Interest Brothers, and have rather a large connection in the fancy goods way. Literally speaking, I am always wandering here and there from my rooms in Covent-garden, London—now about the city streets: now, about the country by-roads—seeing many little things and some great things, which, because they interest me, I think may interest others.

If Dickens' initial adoption of the picaresque mode was primarily determined by his boyhood reading of Cervantes and Smollett and Fielding, he could hardly have made a choice better suited to his purposes and talents. This form has been called the novel of successive encounters; and surely the great unrelated scenes of comedy and melodrama are the passages from Dickens' early stories which remain memorable. That, indeed, he constructed his narratives to link these scenes is apparent from the accompanying illustrations, the subjects of which were customarily specified by the writer. Examples crowd to mind: Pickwick in the Pound, the death of Sikes, the breaking up of Dotheboys Hall, Dick Swiveller teaching cribbage to the Marchioness, Sarah Gamp and Betsey Prig over tea. Not surprisingly Dickens was to find that the material most readily adaptable for public reading came from the earlier works. When, on the other hand, he wanted to carve out a section from *David Copperfield*, he ran into problems which he described to Forster as follows: "There is still the huge difficulty that I constructed the whole with intense pains and have so woven it up and blended it together, that I cannot yet so separate the parts as to tell the story of David's life with Dora." It has not been sufficiently remarked that the episodic nature of the picaresque tale was ideally suited as well for displaying the eccentricities in speech and behavior of the comic and grotesque characters who constitute the indisputable triumphs of Dickens' art at this period. Sam Weller or Quilp or Mrs. Gamp or Pecksniff enjoy absolutely free and autonomous existences; to cramp any one within the exigencies of a tightly woven plot would be to deprive him of the opportunities for uninhibited self-expression which are the very principle of his being.

The reader who uncritically abandons himself to the panoramic vagaries of Dickens' first novels will hardly be disposed to linger over the occasional passages of social comment, incisive as these often are. The reforming conscience is present, but still diffused, principally concerned, as Shaw said, with "individual delinquencies, local plague-spots, negligent authorities." Real injustice and oppression occur within a framework of melodramatically contrived incidents. The victims suffer under private rancor which, as in the case of Monks' persecution of Oliver or Ralph Nickleby's of Kate, is preposterously motivated. The evil-doing of the villains is countered by the equally gratuitous benevolence of such characters as Brownlow, the Cheeryble brothers, and Garland. The distance which Dickens had yet to travel to achieve the sustained satire of his final period can be gauged by contrasting the sporadic incursion of social criticism into his early novels with the full development of the same themes later on. Thus, Pickwick's brief incarceration in the Fleet looks forward to the Marshalsea setting which dominates so much of the action in *Little Dorrit*. Both *Nicholas Nickleby* and *Hard Times* take off from schoolroom scenes; but Squeers' brutal regime at Dotheboys Hall lacks the thematic relevance of Gradgrind's Benthamite institution. The horrors of the industrial landscape to which Nell is fleetingly exposed are little more than a preliminary sketch for the spiritual wasteland of Coketown in *Hard Times*.

Evil always darkens the world of Dickens' fiction; but the novelist was at the outset of his career more occupied with its effects than its causes. Suffering is visited on characters who are both defenseless and blameless, and whose plight, therefore, elicits a primarily emotional response. The forlorn child protagonists of *Oliver Twist* and *The Old Curiosity Shop*, and the idiot Barnaby Rudge sound depths of pathos better calculated to stir the sympathies than to awaken the critical intelligence.

Not before the mid-1840s did Dickens begin to view society in its organic wholeness, and so to perceive the importance of grouping individual lives within encompassing cultural patterns. This was a decade of extreme political and economic unrest, when the populace first felt the full oppression of the Industrial Revolution. *Barnaby Rudge* is the first of Dickens' novels to evince a consistent awareness of contemporary problems. The widespread apprehension aroused by the Chartist agitation for parliamentary reform is mirrored in the treatment of the mob scenes, even though these ostensibly describe the Gordon Riots of 1780. The American episodes in *Martin Chuzzlewit* further illustrate Dickens' growing recognition of the power of society over its individual members. Those would-be individualists, Colonel Diver, Jefferson Brick, LaFayette Kettle, General Cyrus Choke, the Hon. Elijah Pogram, and Hannibal Chollop share a common identity in their blatantly nationalistic prejudices.

With *Dombey and Son* the dynamic operation of change on the life of the age begins to dominate Dickens' imagination. In the railways, spreading their network from city to city across the face of England, the novelist found an emblem for the innovating spirit which had overnight replaced the leisurely world of stagecoaches and country inns celebrated in *Pickwick Papers*. Although too lengthy for quotation, the description of Todgers's immemorial disorderliness in Chapter 9 of *Martin Chuzzlewit* should be compared with the description in Chapter 6 of *Dombey and Son* of the very different kind of disorder visited on Staggs's Gardens by the coming of the railroad. In Todgers's the past is inviolably preserved in the present; the scene from the ensuing novel asserts that today is only prelude to tomorrow. Equally suggestive is the contrast between the great commercial firm of which Dombey is the head and those piratical ventures belonging to a precapitalist era of which Dickens makes sport in *Nicholas Nickleby* and *Martin Chuzzlewit* under the ludicrous appellations of the United Metropolitan Improved Hot Muffin and Crumpet Baking and Punctual Delivery Company, and the Anglo-Bengalee Disinterested Loan and Life Assurance Company.

Both Ralph Nickleby and Montague Tigg are entrepreneurs, and, as such, assignable to no fixed social station. Dombey, on the other hand, is a pillar of middle-class respectability, and his inordinate pride is inseparable from his social position. Along with its emphasis on change, then, *Dombey and Son* shows Dickens' growing insight into the class structure of Victorian society. To such characters as Pickwick and the Cheeryble brothers, material possessions imply no privilege beyond the opportunity to dispense charity, and they treat their beneficiaries as equals. Dombey is the progenitor of a long line of figures in later novels for whom wealth has become the symbol of status, conferring the right to oppress the less fortunate. Variations on the type are Bounderby, Merdle, and Podsnap. William Dorrit joins this company when he inherits his fortune and is able to translate into actuality his playacting in the role of Father of the Marshalsea. Boffin and his wife are Dickens' agents for ridiculing respectively the snobbish aspiration for culture and the love of fashionable display which accompany newly gained riches. Altogether more biting in its reflection on Podsnappery, however, is the miserly pretense which the Golden Dustman assumes to bring Bella Wilfer to her senses. An article from *Blackwood's Magazine* for 1855, quoted by Humphry House, perceptively attributes the novelist's success to his understanding of the capitalist mentality, but seems curiously obtuse in suggesting that Dickens was temperamentally sympathetic with that habit of mind:

We cannot but express our conviction that it is to the fact that he represents a class that he owes his speedy elevation to the top of the wave of popular favour. He is a man of very liberal sentiments—an assailer of constituted wrongs and authorities—one of the advocates in the plea of Poor *versus* Rich, to the progress of which he has lent no small aid in his day. But he is, notwithstanding, perhaps more distinctly than any other author of the time, a *class* writer, the historian and representative of one circle in the many ranks of our social scale. Despite their descents into the lowest class, and their occasional flights into the less familiar ground of fashion, it is the air and breath of middle-class respectability which fills the books of Mr. Dickens.

In the novels written during the 1850s Dickens came increasingly to associate everything he found amiss in the world about him with the concentration of power in the monied middle class. Institutions which had traditionally existed to safeguard the general welfare seemed to him to have passed into the hands of vested interests, committed to perpetuating rather than reforming existing evils. Beginning with *Bleak House*, the writer set out to strip away the hypocritical façades masking the abuse of authority in high places. His blanket term for the monopoly of power by privileged groups was the "System." In a moment of lucidity Gridley, the litigant from Shropshire, makes the following despairing comment on the toils of Chancery which have enmeshed him:

The system! I am told, on all hands, it's the system. I mustn't look to individuals. It's the system. I mustn't go into Court, and say, "My Lord, I beg to know this from you—is this right or wrong? Have you the face to tell me I have received justice, and therefore am dismissed?" My Lord knows nothing of it. He sits there, to administer the system. . . . I will accuse the individual workers of that system against me, face to face, before the great eternal bar!

Society in its institutionalized aspect has replaced the individual malefactors of the early novels as the true villain.

Dickens' scorn for the governing class dated from his days as a journalist, when he reported the parliamentary debates leading up to the passage of the Reform Bill of 1832. During the subsequent decades his pessimism was accentuated by a variety of factors: the ineptitude of legislative attempts to deal with the distress brought on by the Industrial Revolution, the disillusionment of his tour in America, the influence of Carlyle's antidemocratic writings. In 1854 the novelist was proclaiming his "hope to have every man in England feel something of the contempt for the House of Commons that I have." And the following year after the Crimean debacle he stated:

I am hourly strengthened in my old belief that our political aristocracy and our tuft-hunting are the death of England. In all this business I don't see a gleam of hope. As to the popular spirit, it has come to be so entirely separated from the Parliament and Government, and so perfectly apathetic about them both, that I seriously think it a most portentous sign.

This attitude dictated the brilliant parody of party faction in *Bleak House*, with its portrayal of the " 'oodle-ites" and the " 'uffy-ites" maneuvering for the spoils of office. Broader based and more searching in its implications is the mockery in *Little Dorrit* of the Circumlocution Office under the domination of Lord Decimus Tite Barnacle and his parasitic clan. Dickens' political satire culminates in the chapter in *Our Mutual Friend* describing how the upstart Veneering bribes his way into Parliament with the wealth derived from wildcat speculation in corporation shares.

Early experience had left Dickens with as little respect for the legal profession as for politicians. With rare exceptions, such as Jaggers in *Great Expectations*, the attorneys in his novels discredit their calling. They are the venal and frequently fraudulent supporters of the established order, masters of prevarication and double-dealing. The "Wiglomeration" against which John Jarndyce rails is their natural element. Many of Dickens' most memorable scenes from *Pickwick Papers* to *A Tale of Two Cities* take place in courtrooms and make fun of legal procedures. *Bleak House,* however, contains Dickens' most concentrated attack on this form of institutionalized chicanery. The lineaments of Tulkinghorn, Vholes, Conversation Kenge, and Guppy are carefully differentiated, but all make their living off Chancery and have a common interest in preserving that outworn relic. The blighting effect of the case of Jarndyce and Jarndyce on the lives of its innocent victims is conveyed in the catalogue of names for Miss Flite's birds, which swells to a crescendo of wild humor: "Hope, Joy, Youth, Peace, Rest, Life, Dust, Ashes, Waste, Want, Ruin, Despair, Madness, Death, Cunning, Folly, Words, Wigs, Rags, Sheepskin, Plunder, Precedent, Jargon, Gammon, and Spinach."

In the world of Dickens' novels the irresponsibility of religious bodies matches that of the law. The nonconforming sects in particular aroused the writer's animus, and he took savage delight in pillorying such canting hypocrites as Stiggins, the Reverend Melchisedech Howler, and Chadband. Although always ready to enroll his name in support of legitimate causes, Dickens recognized that too often organized philanthropy was only incidentally occupied with its professed goals. The fashionable sponsorship of charitable enterprises calls forth from Boffin a memorable tirade; and the type of professional "do-gooder" is scathingly anatomized in *Bleak House.* The rapaciously benevolent Mrs. Pardiggle, forcing her Puseyite tracts on the bricklayer and his family, is as little mindful of their true needs as Mrs. Jellyby, immersed in schemes for the colonization of Borioboola-Gha, is attentive to her domestic duties.

Dickens shared the belief of all leading Victorian reformers that more and better education was requisite if the lower classes were to be helped to better their condition; but he also perceived that the delegated authorities used educational reform as an excuse for regimenting the minds of pupils, indoctrinating them with class prejudice and instilling an uncritical acceptance of debased values. Along with those like Paul Dombey and David Copperfield who suffer under outmoded methods of instruction, he created a gallery of youths spoiled by more progressive schooling. Included in this category are Rob the Grinder, Uriah Heep, Bitzer and Tom Gradgrind, and Charley Hexam. The descriptions of the teaching in Gradgrind's school and in the Ragged School which young Hexam attended are object lessons in how young minds are sacrificed to the application of pet theories.

Sometimes Dickens' heart leads him astray, and he presents a misleading view of the institution he is satirizing. Forster truthfully observed that "he had not made politics at any time a study, and they were always an instinct with him rather than a science." A case in point is the novelist's persistent failure to do justice to the programs for reform supported by the Philosophic Radicals. The Benthamites' dislike of administrative inefficiency and their passion for systematizing obscured his eyes to the deeply humanitarian spirit which prompted the efforts of these thinkers to ameliorate existing evils. Thus, the sympathy aroused for Oliver Twist's hard lot in a badly run workhouse makes no allowance for the fact that the Poor Law of 1834 was enacted to do away with the much greater hardships of outdoor relief. By the same token, the reader of *Hard Times* can hardly be expected to infer that the parliamentary blue books on Gradgrind's shelves contain the reports of responsible and public-spirited governmental committees created to investigate the insufferable living and working conditions of the industrial populace.

Dickens was always generous in giving credit to social agencies whose benefactions he had observed. He ardently supported the great work of Shaftesbury and Chadwick on the General Board of Health. It has been pointed out that his legal satire does not extend to the bench, although it includes unpaid magistrates like Fang in *Oliver Twist*, modeled on a notorious original. In the slumworker, Frank Milvey of *Our Mutual Friend*, and the jolly Muscular Christian, Canon Crisparkle in *The Mystery of Edwin Drood*, Dickens presented types of churchmen unselfishly devoted to their clerical duties. From first-hand experience the novelist admired the even-handed maintenance of law and order by the Metropolitan Police; and an Inspector Field of the Detective Department was the model for the admirable Bucket in *Bleak House*, generally accounted the first sleuth in English fiction. The setting for Johnny's death in *Our Mutual Friend* was based on the Hospital for Sick Children in Great Ormond Street. In 1858 Dickens was the principal speaker at a banquet which raised £3000 for this foundation.

The accusation is often lodged that Dickens' social criticism, for all its cogency, is largely negative in tendency. The Utilitarian Harriet Martineau was among the first to take the novelist to task for the absence of constructive proposals in his writings, even while she granted their immense prestige. In her *History of the Thirty Years' Peace* she wrote:

It is scarcely conceivable that anyone should, in our age of the world, exert a stronger social influence than Mr. Dickens has in his power. His sympathies are on the side of the suffering and the frail; and this makes him the idol of those who suffer, from whatever cause. We may wish that he had a sounder social philosophy, and that he could suggest a loftier moral to sufferers. . . .

In rebuttal one can argue that through legislative and other means the Victorian age amended the worst offenses to which Dickens was among the first to draw attention, and that his writings demonstrably contributed to this betterment. Nevertheless, the charge is not really relevant, since it derives from a misapprehension both of Dickens' habit of mind and of his artistic purposes.

At no time did Dickens espouse any narrowly doctrinaire position; and all attempts to associate him with a school of political philosophy, whether Benthamite, Socialist, or Marxist, seriously distort his message. The London *Times* was nearer the mark in calling him "pre-eminently a writer of the people and for the people . . . the 'Great Commoner' of English fiction." Like Cobbett in the preceding and Carlyle and Ruskin in his own generation, his iconoclasm is of a peculiarly British stamp, an emotional blend of traditional and revolutionary elements without regard for intellectual consistency. In the term which he often used of himself, Dickens is perhaps best described as a "radical." Humphry House, who noted that this designation was still vaguely defined in the novelist's time, suggests that "by so often arrogating it to himself he helped to extend its application to cover almost any person whose sympathies, whenever occasion offered, were with the under-dog." House's opinion receives confirmation from Anthony Trollope's statement: "If any man ever was so, he was a radical at heart, believing entirely in the people, writing for them, speaking for them. . . ." Radicalism so interpreted sets the proper context for Dickens' frequently misunderstood summary of his political faith, uttered in the year before he died to the Birmingham and Midland Institute: "My faith in the people governing is, on the whole, infinitesimal; my faith in the People governed is, on the whole, illimitable."

As a novelist, Dickens' concern was with characters, not principles. This is simply to say that he did not think of himself as a practical reformer, responsible for advocating specific measures to eliminate the evils he deplored, but rather as a moralist whose mission was to lay bare the origins of those evils in prevalent attitudes of heart and mind. As early as 1838 a writer in the *Edinburgh Review* correctly identified the purport of Dickens' teaching:

One of the qualities we most admire in him is his comprehensive spirit of humanity. The tendency of his writings is to make us practically benevolent—to excite our sympathy in behalf of the aggrieved and suffering in all classes; and especially in those who are most removed from observation. . . . His humanity is plain, practical, and manly. It is quite untainted with sentimentality.

Through his fiction Dickens aimed at arousing the conscience of his age. To his success in doing so, a Nonconformist preacher paid the following tribute: "There have been at work among us three great social agencies: the London City Mission; the novels of Mr. Dickens; the cholera."

The moral purpose which sustains Dickens' work from beginning to end is voiced by Marley's ghost in "A Christmas Carol." In response to Scrooge's assertion that he was "always a good man of business," the ghost cries: "Business! . . . Mankind was my business. The common welfare was my business; charity, mercy, forbearance, and benevolence, were, all, my business. The dealings of my trade were but a drop of water in the comprehensive ocean of my business!" The Dickensian ideal of community spirit is perhaps most ap-

pealingly embodied in the Christmas festivities at Ding-
ley Dell, or in the humbler celebration of the same
holiday by the Cratchit family. Such scenes led the
French critic Cazamian to attribute to the author what
he called "la philosophie de Noël," suggestive of a
hearty but vague social altruism. In the early novels
this doctrine is promulgated by a series of Santa Claus
figures: Pickwick himself, Brownlow, the Cheeryble
brothers, Garland, and old Martin Chuzzlewit. Gissing
bitingly characterized these stories as presenting a
"world of eccentric benevolence," in which the author's "saviour of society was a man of heavy purse
and large heart, who did the utmost possible good in
his own particular sphere."

Apart from the ministrations of such benign *dei ex
machina*, however, Dickens looked primarily to the
lower classes for evidences of that sense of kinship
which represents his social ideal. In *The Old Curiosity
Shop* he writes: ". . . if ever household affections and
loves are graceful things, they are graceful in the poor.
The ties that bind the wealthy and the proud to home
may be forged on earth, but those which link the poor
man to his humble hearth are of the truer metal and
bear the stamp of Heaven." Throughout the novels
there occur scenes of shared family life among the
lowly and unpretending which mordantly reflect on
the divisive effects of wealth and social station. Such
little refuges of domestic harmony in their respective
stories include the homes of the Toodles in *Dombey and
Son*, the Peggottys in *David Copperfield*, and the Plor-
nishes in *Little Dorrit*. But for Dickens the instinctual
sympathies uniting the poor transcend the bonds of
blood, and never manifest themselves more strongly
than in times of hardship and distress, again in contrast
to the selfish behavior of members of the privileged
classes in like situations. Addressing the Metropolitan

Sanitary Association in 1850, Dickens said: "No one who had any experience of the poor could fail to be deeply affected by their patience, by their sympathy with one another, and by the beautiful alacrity with which they helped each other in toil, in the day of suffering, and at the hour of death." One recalls the devotion of Liz and Jenny, the brickmakers' wives in *Bleak House*, or the way the hands in *Hard Times* turn out to help rescue Stephen Blackpool from the mine-shaft. Of the disreputable circus performers in the same novel, Dickens writes: "Yet there was a remarkable gentleness and childishness about these people, a special inaptitude for any kind of sharp practice, and an untiring readiness to help and pity one another. . . ."

The satiric intent which so uniformly underlies Dickens' social criticism, however, tends to put what he was against in bolder relief than what he was for. Whether manifested in political and economic terms as the "cash-nexus" of laissez-faire capitalism, or in religious terms as the smug self-righteousness of the Protestant ethos, or in social terms as ostentatious class snobbery, the temper of the age is subsumed for Dickens under the one all-pervasive vice of egoism. To Forster the novelist wrote of his despair for the future of a people enslaved to the doctrine of "everybody for himself and nobody for the rest." He displays this habit of mind in all its meanness in the parody of Utilitarian ethics by means of which Fagin brings Noah Claypole to heel. To avoid the gallows, says the Jew to his creature:

you depend upon me. To keep my little business all snug, I depend upon you. The first is your number one, the second my number one. The more you value your number one, the more careful you must be of mine; so we come at last to what I told you at first—that a regard for number one holds us all together, and must do so, unless we would all go to pieces in company.

Selfishness, which provides the organizing theme of *Martin Chuzzlewit*, conditions the behavior of other characters as formidable in their capacity to inflict unhappiness on their dependents as Bounderby, Mrs. Clennam, and Podsnap. All of Dickens' real villains are ruthlessly bent on their own interests. None represents the type better than the sinister Blandois of *Little Dorrit*, who cynically invokes the way of the world to justify his scheming. Asked by Clennam whether he sells all his friends, he answers: "I sell anything that commands a price. How do your lawyers live, your politicians, your intriguers, your men of the Exchange? . . . Effectively, sir, Society sells itself and sells me: and I sell Society."

In Dickens' presentation this dog-eat-dog philosophy has extinguished the very principle of communal concern, leaving the weak perpetually at the mercy of the strong. Oliver Twist's words, while he is being led to Sowerberry's undertaking establishment, so poignantly dramatize the helplessness of the unprotected that even Bumble is momentarily abashed: "I will be good indeed; indeed, indeed I will, sir! I am a very little boy, sir; and it is so—so— . . . So lonely, sir! So very lonely!" The novelist habitually chooses children and distressed members of the working class to awaken moral outrage against the kinds of oppression visited by society on its defenseless members. And this oppression is most destructive of human dignity when it assumes an institutional form; for then it operates with complete impersonality, treating its victims like soulless objects. Thus, Jo, the crossing-sweeper of *Bleak House*, is always being "moved on" by authorities who do not know what to do with him, except when he is being treated as a pawn for self-interested ends which are unintelligible to him. He is so used by Tulkinghorn, by Chadband, by Lady Dedlock, by Bucket, by Skimpole. In the same way Stephen Blackpool in *Hard Times*, having successively served his purpose as a butt for the labor-agitator Slackbridge and for his employer Bounderby, is cast off by both to become Tom Gradgrind's tool. Stephen's dying prayer "that aw th' world may on'y coom toogether more, an' get a better unnerstan'in o' one another," is, under the circumstances, a charitable arraignment of the appalling inhumanity under which so many individuals suffer in Dickens' novels.

From the disintegration of all traditions making for social cohesiveness in an age so given over to self-aggrandizement not even the family is immune. Dickens' portraits of hard-hearted parents, it has been suggested, are a reflection of his own bitterness against his father and mother for abandoning him during a crucial period in his boyhood. However this may be, the neglected children in his novels are perhaps less to be pitied than those who are callously exploited to further their parents' own selfish ends. Among those who traffic in the love of sons and daughters, sometimes but by no means always under the pretext of altruism, are Mr. Dombey and Mrs. Skewton in *Dombey and Son*, Turveydrop, Mrs. Jellyby, and Skimpole in *Bleak House*, Gradgrind in *Hard Times*, William Dorrit in *Little Dorrit*, and Gaffer Hexam and Mr. Dolls in *Our Mutual Friend*.

The hardships afflicting so large a part of the populace in the Victorian era produced, in reaction, an extensive and eloquent body of social criticism. Dickens' denunciation of filth and ignorance, as well as of the lack of responsible attention to those conditions and the degradation resulting therefrom, adds nothing substantially to the preachments of Carlyle and Ruskin, and the other great reformers who were his contemporaries. Furthermore, the reader in search of factual information about conditions in the slums and factories will find fuller documentation in the work of novelists who wrote with a more obtrusively didactic purpose. As tracts for the times Disraeli's *Sybil*, Kingsley's *Alton Locke*, and Mrs. Gaskell's *Mary Barton* and *North and South* possess greater sociological value than Dickens' novels.* Yet, these novels achieve an imaginative amplitude absent from more programmatically realistic treatments of the contemporary scene. For at the heart of Dickens' endeavor lay the profound conviction that man does not live by bread alone, that physical well-being is not enough if unilluminated by the vision of higher things. A piece in *Household Words*, entitled "The Amusements of the People," and written at the time of the Great Exhibition, summarizes the author's belief: "There is a range of imagination in most of us, which no amount of steam-engines will satisfy; and which The-great-exhibition-of-the-works-of-industry-of-all-nations, itself, will probably leave unappeased." He wrote in *Hard Times*:

The poor you will have always with you. Cultivate in them, while there is yet time, the utmost graces of the fancies and affections, to adorn their lives so much in need of adornment; or, in the day of your triumph, when romance is utterly driven out of their souls, and they and a bare existence stand face to face, Reality will take a wolfish turn, and make an end of you.

In contrast to other Victorian novels with a social purpose, Dickens' writings convey a sense of the pres-

* Dickens, of course, reserved his most forthright pronouncements on existing evils for his speeches and the pages of *Household Words* and *All the Year Round*.

sure of environment on the inner, as well as the outer, lives of the characters. The reader learns not only what life was like in the world portrayed, but how it really *felt* to have to live in such a world. Especially in the later stories, the moral atmosphere is polarized by at one extreme the hopeless despair of the lower classes, and at the other the hard-hearted complacency regnant throughout the middle class. The two tempers of mind combine to create an impression of joyless apathy, indicative of that paralysis of the social will which for Dickens seemed increasingly to be the true *mal de siècle*.

A scene from "The Chimes," the Christmas story for 1844, illustrates in brief Dickens' sense of how the theories of the political economists reduced human nature to a bloodless abstraction. This is the passage in which the Malthusian statistician converts to feelings of guilt Trotty Veck's innocent pleasure in his luncheon of tripe. Later in the same tale Fern speaks for the author in voicing the workingman's plea for social justice; and it is noteworthy that he does not stop with the need for better living conditions, but goes on to lay the blame for class antagonism to the systematic neglect or abuse by those in authority of all ties promoting community of interest. Dickens was making much the same point ten years later when, after a visit to the strike-bound town of Preston in preparation for writing *Hard Times*, he declared in *Household Words* that "political economy is a mere skeleton unless it has a little human covering and filling out, a little human bloom upon it, and a little human warmth in it."

On much the same grounds Dickens scorned the sectarian spirit in religion. In summarizing the articles of his own simple faith, he wrote to a clergyman on Christmas Eve 1856:

There cannot be many men, I believe, who have a more humble veneration for the New Testament, or a more profound conviction of its all-sufficiency, than I have. If I am ever . . . mistaken on this subject, it is because I discountenance all obtrusive professions of and tradings in religion, as one of the main causes why real Christianity has been retarded in this world; and because my observation of life induces me to hold in unspeakable dread and horror, those unseemly squabbles about the letter which drive the spirit out of hundreds of thousands.

The failure of religion to redeem the age from materialism Dickens laid especially to the inherence in the middle class of that sour Puritanical strain which equates salvation with worldly prosperity. Cheerless itself, it was bent on suppressing the instinct for joy in others. The type is most memorably presented in the guilt-ridden and life-denying Mrs. Clennam of *Little Dorrit*. Arthur Clennam places her among those whose "religion was a gloomy sacrifice of tastes and sympathies that were never their own, offered up as a part of a bargain for the security of their possessions. Austere faces, inexorable discipline, penance in this world and terror in the next—nothing graceful or gentle anywhere. . . ." For Dickens the dismal gloom of Sundays in London epitomized all that was most forbidding in the religious temper of Victorian England. As far back as 1830 he had written under the pseudonym of Timothy Sparks a fervid pamphlet, entitled "Sunday under Three Heads: As it is; As Sabbath Bills would make it; As it might be." The immediate occasion for this diatribe was Sir Andrew Agnew's Sunday Observance Bill, which the writer regarded as a conspiratorial measure on the part of the governing classes to deprive the populace of its one day in the week of carefree pleasure.

Despite his advocacy of mass education, Dickens found that too many systems of education, whether sponsored by the state or the church, operated on the same killjoy principles. At a dinner for the Warehousemen and Clerks' Schools in 1857 he denounced all schools

where the bright childish imagination is utterly discouraged, and where those bright childish faces, which it is so very good for the wisest among us to remember in after life, when the world is too much with us early and late, are gloomily and grimly scared out of countenance; where I have never seen among the pupils, whether boys or girls, anything but little parrots and small calculating machines.

In another address the following year he developed his educational ideals with reference to Christ's manner of teaching: "Knowledge has a very limited power when it informs the head only; but when it informs the heart as well, it has a power over life and death, and body and the soul, and dominates the universe." Doubtless with the rewards of his own early reading in mind, the novelist insisted especially on the importance of nurturing the instinct for wonder in the young. Beginning with "The Mudfog Papers," which appeared in *Bentley's Miscellany* (1837–1838), he persistently satirized the Utilitarian doctrinaires who neglected the fancy in their insistence on the acquisition of factual information. His most masterful treatment of this theme occurs, of course, in *Hard Times*. The textbook definition of the horse which enables Bitzer to show up Sissy Jupe makes no provision for the dancing circus animal that foils his pursuit of Tom Gradgrind. And in the face of the havoc wrought by his educational theories, Mr. Gradgrind is brought humbly to acknowledge the supremacy of Sissy's impulsive wisdom of the heart. Sleary's account of the devotion exhibited by Mr. Jupe's performing dog stands as the final comment on Dickens' meaning. "It theemth," the circus-master says to Gradgrind

to prethent two thingth to a perthon, don't it, Thquire? . . . one, that there ith a love in the world, not all Thelf-interetht after all, but thomething very different; t'other, that it hath a way of ith own of calculating or not calculating, whith thomehow or another ith at leatht ath hard to give a name to, ath the wayth of the dogth ith!

The preliminary notice to *Household Words* set forth the goals which Dickens hoped to realize in his weekly:

No mere utilitarian spirit, no iron binding of the mind to grim realities, will give a harsh tone to our *Household Words*. In the bosoms of the young and old, of the well-to-do and of the poor, we would tenderly cherish that light of Fancy which is inherent in the human breast; which, according to its nurture, burns with an inspiring flame, or sinks into a sullen glare, but which (or woe betide that day!) can never be extinguished. To show to all, that in all familiar things, even in those which are repellent on the surface, there is Romance enough, if we will find it out:—to teach the hardest workers at this whirling wheel of toil, that their lot is not necessarily a moody, brutal fact, excluded from the sympathies and graces of imagination; to bring the greater and the lesser together, upon that wide field, and mutually dispose them to a better acquaintance and kinder understanding— is one main object of our *Household Words*.

The same controlling purpose carried over to *All the Year Round*, in which the editor announced that he would continue to strive for "That fusion of the graces of the imagination with the realities of life, which is vital to the welfare of any community. . . ." A like intent was to the fore in Dickens' fiction. The Preface to *Bleak House* states that in this story he had "purposely dwelt on the romantic side of familiar things." Any estimate, therefore, of the significance of Dickens' novels as social commentary on their age must take into account the author's concept of his dual function as critic and entertainer.

As he clarified his social vision, Dickens at the same time discovered more imaginative means of projecting that vision. Although the discussion of the formal aspects of his achievement properly belongs to the later chapters of this volume, some indications may here be given of how the writer combined extraordinary astuteness in his response to the life of the age with the ability to transmute his observations into themes of enduring relevance. As a result, his work surmounts the limitations of both the *roman social* and the naturalistic novel: the one confined to topicality by its didactic purpose, the other overly literal in its striving for verisimilitude.

Of Dickens' novels, *Bleak House*, *Hard Times*, *Little Dorrit*, and *Our Mutual Friend* are the richest in reference for the student of Victorian life. Scholars have demonstrated the historical accuracy of most of the situations in these stories, whether it be the spreading pestilence of *Bleak House*, the labor unrest in *Hard Times*, or the financial panic in *Little Dorrit*. Yet, the author has so generalized his treatment of contemporary phenomena that they transcend their localized settings. *Bleak House* came out at a time when a series of ministerial crises was underscoring the want of responsible leadership in England; but it is not necessary to have these facts in mind to recognize in the goings on at Chesney Wold a timeless satire on political patronage and the spoils system. Similarly, although the Circumlocution Office in *Little Dorrit* was immediately inspired by the revelation of flagrant mismanagement on the part of all departments entrusted with the conduct of the Crimean War, Dickens' indictment of

bureaucratic red tape and muddleheaded officialdom
has lost none of its cogency.

The novelist's success in harnessing reforming zeal
to artistic ends is perhaps most apparent in his development of associative images. The fog which shrouds the
opening of *Bleak House* by metaphoric expansion embraces the murky procedures of Chancery. In the same
way Old Harmon's dust-mounds in *Our Mutual Friend*,
real enough as a feature of the city landscape, emblem-
atically represent the whole sordid, money-grubbing
basis of capitalist economy. In contrast to the baldly
factual accounts of tenement and factory conditions
provided by other novels of the period, Dickens'
method in *Hard Times* is impressionistic. The description of Coketown does not insist on the unguarded
machinery in the mills or the open sewers under the
dwellings, but rather, evokes the deadening monotony
which was the truly brutalizing element in the lives of
the workers. It is doubtful, however, whether any
amount of naturalistic reportage could impart so in-
delible a sense of the blighting effect of the machine
age on the human spirit as the fanciful breadth of the
following description:

It was a town of red brick, or of brick that would have
been red if the smoke and ashes had allowed it; but as
matters stood it was a town of unnatural red and black
like the painted face of a savage. It was a town of
machinery and tall chimneys, out of which interminable
serpents of smoke trailed themselves for ever and ever, and
never got uncoiled. It had a black canal in it, and a river
that ran purple with ill-smelling dye, and vast piles of
building full of windows where there was a rattling and
trembling all day long, and where the piston of the
steam-engine worked monotonously up and down, like
the head of an elephant in a state of melancholy madness.
It contained several large streets all very like one another,
and many small streets still more like one another, in-

habited by people equally like one another, who all went in and out at the same hours, with the same sound upon the same pavements, to do the same work, and to whom every day was the same as yesterday and to-morrow, and every year the counterpart of the last and the next.

THREE

DICKENS AND
HIS READERS

*The more we see of life and its brevity, and the world
and its varieties, the more we know that no exercise of
our abilities in any art, but
the addressing of it to the*   LETTER FROM CHARLES DICKENS
great ocean of humanity   TO WILLIAM MACREADY
in which we are drops, and   —JANUARY 14, 1853
*not to bye-ponds (very
stagnant) here and there, ever can or ever will lay
the foundations of an endurable retrospect.*

*It leaves me—as my Art always finds and always leaves
me—the most restless of created Beings. I am the modern
embodiment of the old
Enchanters, whose Familiars*   LETTER FROM CHARLES DICKENS
tore them to pieces. I weary   TO MRS. WINTER
of rest, and have no   —DECEMBER 7, 1857
*satisfaction but in fatigue.
Realities and idealities are always comparing
themselves before me. . . .*

*As to my art, I have as great a delight in it as the most
enthusiastic of my readers; and the sense of my trust
and responsibility in that
wise, is always upon me*   LETTER FROM CHARLES DICKENS
when I take pen in hand.   TO ANGELA BURDETT COUTTS
If I were soured, I should   —APRIL 10, 1860
*still try to sweeten the
lives and fancies of others, but I am not—not at all.*

N ARTICLE WRITTEN BY WILKIE COLLINS FOR *HOUSE-HOLD WORDS* IN 1858 CONTAINS THE FOLLOWING OBSERVATIONS ON THE NEW READING PUBLIC WHICH had arisen in the wake of the spread of literacy in Victorian England:

The Unknown Public is, in a literary sense, hardly beginning, as yet, to learn to read. . . . it is perhaps hardly too much to say that the future of English fiction may rest with this Unknown Public, which is now waiting to be taught the difference between a good book and a bad. It is probably a question of time only. . . . When that period comes, the readers who rank by millions, will be the readers who give the widest reputations, who return the richest awards, and who will, therefore, command the service of the best writers of their time. A great, an unparalleled prospect awaits, perhaps, the coming generation of English novelists. To the penny journals of the present times belongs the credit of having discovered a new public. When that public shall discover its need of a great writer, tne great writer will have such an audience as has never yet been known.

Yet, twenty years earlier Dickens had already captured this audience; indeed, the success of his early writings may be said to have called attention to its existence. A well-known anecdote illustrates the envying wonder with which contemporary writers acknowledged his supremacy. Thackeray, then at work on *Vanity Fair*, greeted the fifth number of *Dombey and Son* with this comment: "There's no writing against such power as this—One has no chance! Read that chapter describing young Paul's death: it is unsurpassed—it is stupendous!"

After *Pickwick Papers* took hold, the sales of monthly installments rarely fell below 25,000, and averaged between 30,000 and 40,000. While *The Old Curiosity Shop* was running, the weekly circulation of *Master Humphrey's Clock* rose to 100,000; and *Great Expectations* pushed the circulation of *All the Year Round* well above that of the London *Times*. These figures, of course, do not take into account the continuing popularity of the novels in book form, whether in the original editions or in cheaper reprints. A fourth printing of *Great Expectations*, for example, was called for within a few weeks of its publication in covers; and more than four million copies of the novels were sold in the twelve years following the author's death. It has been estimated that during his lifetime Dickens addressed an audience of a million and a half, or approximately one out of ten readers in Great Britain. There is no way of guessing the numbers of the illiterate for whom the writer's name was a household word. Forster recounts a delightfully informative episode of 1847, relating to a visit by the novelist to one of his sons who was ill with scarlet fever in the home of his grandmother:

An elderly charwoman employed about the place had shown so much sympathy in the family trouble, that Mrs. Hogarth especially told her of the approaching visit, and who it was that was coming to the sick-room. "Lawk ma'am!" she said. "Is the young gentleman upstairs the son of the man that put together *Dombey*?" Reassured upon this point, she explained her question by declaring that she never thought there was a man that *could* have put together *Dombey*. Being pressed farther as to what her notion was of this mystery of a *Dombey* (for it was known that she could not read), it turned out that she lodged at a snuff-shop kept by a person named Douglas, where there were several other lodgers; and that on the first Monday of every month there was a Tea, and the landlord read the month's number of *Dombey*, those only of the lodgers who subscribed to the tea partaking of that luxury, but all having the benefit of the reading; and the impression produced on the old charwoman revealed itself in the remark with which she closed her account of it. "Lawk, ma'am! I thought that three or four men must have put together *Dombey*!"

Dickens did not simply welcome, he courted popular acclaim. The satisfactions of artistic repute and financial gain must not be discounted; but the novelist's endeavors to get on more and more intimate terms with his audience involved, as well, psychological factors. Although he was at all times uncommunicative about his literary habits, much may be inferred from his reliance on the stimuli provided by the amateur theatricals and public readings in which he successively engaged. According to Otis Skinner, when the novelist one day expressed to his protégé Edmund Yates regret that he had not made a career on the stage, and when the young man pointed out that he was, after all, a great writer, Dickens answered: "That's all very well, but I would rather have been a great actor and had the public at my feet." To a friend, Mrs. Watson, he confessed the gratification he had derived from playing the lead in Wilkie Collins' melodrama, *The Frozen Deep:*

All last summer I had a transitory satisfaction in rending the very heart out of my body by doing that Richard

Wardour part. It was a good thing to have a couple of thousand people all rigid and frozen together, in the palm of one's hand—as at Manchester—and to see the hardened carpenters at the sides crying and trembling at it night after night.

The sense of fulfillment which Dickens found in theatrical make-believe cannot be disassociated from his literary career. In a letter of 1857 to the artist Daniel Maclise, again with reference to his part in *The Frozen Deep*, the novelist declared: "In that perpetual struggle after an expression of the truth . . . the interest of such a character to me is that it enables me, as it were, *to write a book in company* instead of in my own solitary room and to feel its effect coming freshly back upon me from the reader." Mary Dickens reported a remarkable scene, indicative not only of her father's close identification with his characters, but also of the manner in which they sprang dramatically to life as their creator enacted their roles on the stage of his imagination. The young girl, who had been admitted to Dickens' study while she was recuperating from an illness, recalled in after years:

On one of these mornings, I was lying on a sofa endeavoring to keep perfectly quiet, while my father wrote busily and rapidly at his desk, when he suddenly jumped up from his chair and rushed to a mirror which hung near and in which I could see the reflection of some extraordinary facial contortions which he was making. He returned rapidly to his desk, wrote furiously for a few moments, and then went again to the mirror. The facial pantomime was resumed, and then turning toward, but evidently not seeing me, he began talking in a low voice. Ceasing this soon, however, he returned once more to his desk, where he remained silently writing until luncheon time.

Dickens' hope that the paid readings would lead to a still closer rapport with his public was amply realized. Shortly after the start of the second series in 1861, he wrote to Forster: ". . . everywhere I have found that peculiar personal relation between my audience and myself on which I counted most when I entered on this enterprise." These performances, however, were prompted by an additional motive which Dickens was perhaps more reluctant to admit, one which had its origin, as did his mesmeric experiments, in the will to dominate. At the end of December 1844 he made a flying trip from Italy to London in order to read aloud to an inner circle of friends his new Christmas book, "The Chimes." In describing this session, he jubilantly wrote to his wife: "If you had seen Macready [the great Shakespearean actor-manager] last night undisguisedly sobbing, and crying on the sofa as I read, you would have felt, as I did, what a thing it is to have power." There can be no doubt that in undertaking against the advice of his closest associates the violently emotional rendition of Sikes' murder of Nancy which hastened his death, Dickens wanted to test the full extent of his sway over the feelings of his auditors. To Forster he announced the new performance in the following terms:

I have made a short reading of the murder in *Oliver Twist*. I cannot make up my mind, however, whether to do it or not. I have no doubt that I could perfectly petrify an audience by carrying out the notion I have of the way of rendering it. But whether the impression would not be so horrible as to keep them away another time, is what I cannot satisfy myself upon.

All evidence points to the fact that Dickens became in a manner possessed by the role and that he derived a guilty pleasure from night after night working up his audience to the requisite pitch of terror. A friend was invited to the first performance in these words: "Come early in January, and see a certain friend of yours do the murder from Oliver Twist. It is horribly like, I am afraid! I have a vague sensation of being 'wanted' as I walk about the streets." Writing to an American friend, he further amplified his involvement in the part:

I begin to doubt and fear on the subject of your having a horror of me after seeing the murder. I don't think a hand moved while I was doing it last night, or an eye looked away. And there was a fixed expression of horror of me, all over the theatre, which could not have been surpassed if I had been going to be hanged to that red velvet table. It is quite a new sensation to be execrated with that unanimity; and I hope it will remain so!

All of Dickens' novels made their first appearance in serial form. Nine came out in monthly installments: *Pickwick Papers, Nicholas Nickleby, Martin Chuzzlewit, Dombey and Son, David Copperfield, Bleak House, Little Dorrit, Our Mutual Friend,* and *The Mystery of Edwin Drood.** Five were composed for weekly serialization: *The Old Curiosity Shop* and *Barnaby Rudge* in *Master Humphrey's Clock; Hard Times* in *Household Words;* and *A Tale of Two Cities†* and *Great Expectations* in *All the Year Round.*

* Dickens' last novel, only six parts of which were written, was to be completed in twelve, instead of the usual twenty monthly parts.

† This story, also issued in monthly parts, illustrates the author's shrewdness in bidding for the widest possible audience. Dickens wrote to Forster that he had "struck out a rather original and bold idea. That is, at the end of each month to publish the monthly part in the green cover, with the two illustrations, at the old shilling. This will give *All the Year Round* always the interest and precedence of a fresh weekly

Oliver Twist appeared in the monthly issues of *Bentley's Miscellany* which Dickens was editing at the time. Although he took up the weekly form with the intention of getting into more frequent correspondence with his readers, Dickens never ceased to fret under the restrictions of tailoring his narrative into briefer segments; and indeed, with *Hard Times* he returned to the practice of blocking out his stories as if for monthly installments. Thus, the novelist's preferred and characteristic method was that of monthly serialization, calling, as he said, for "the large canvas and the big brushes."

Most serious novels, when Dickens began to write, appeared in three volumes. These "three-deckers" normally sold for a half-guinea a volume, a prohibitively high price for those who could not afford to subscribe to circulating libraries. At a shilling a number Dickens' works commanded a significantly wider market. The green-covered parts, issued on the last day of each month, contained exactly thirty-two pages of text (three or four chapters), accompanied by two illustrations. There were nineteen parts in all, since the last was a double issue of sixty-four pages and with four illustrations, selling for two shillings. Included in the final installment was a frontispiece, title page, preface, and other introductory matter, so that the entire work could be bound in book form.

In the announcement (1847) of the "Cheap" or People's Edition of his works, Dickens asserted that the shilling monthly numbers were "a very unusual form" when he adopted it at the outset of his career. It was known to him, as he wrote in the Preface to *Pickwick*

portion during the month; and will give me my old standing with my old public, and the advantage (very necessary in this story) of having numbers of people who read it in no portions smaller than a monthly part."

Papers, through "a dim recollection of certain interminable novels in that form, which used to be carried
about the country by peddlers, and over some of which
I remember to have shed innumerable tears before I
had served my apprenticeship to Life." Actually the
mode had been successfully used in series of sketches
of sporting and low life by Pierce Egan, the most
popular of which was entitled *Life in London* (1821).
This work, however, made its appeal principally
through Cruikshank's illustrations, as was intended to
be the case when Dickens was first invited to col-
laborate with Seymour on *Pickwick Papers*. Dickens
was thus taking over a relatively untried medium,
flexible enough to call forth his originality and to
stimulate the free exercise of his imaginative resources.

The drawbacks of adhering to a rigorous schedule
and of producing the precise amount of copy necessary
to fill out thirty-two pages were for Dickens more
than counterbalanced by the sense of immediate audience participation which he derived from serial publication. Unlike other novelists who were unwilling to
commit to print unfinished manuscripts, he rarely had
a backlog of more than three or four numbers when
the works began to appear, and before long he was
hard pressed to keep up with the typesetters' monthly
deadline. The sales of parts Dickens regarded as a kind
of barometer registering the periodic fluctuations in
his reputation. One of his reasons for sending young
Martin Chuzzlewit to the United States, as has been
said, was the hope that a change in locale might revive
lagging interest in that story.

Dickens' dependence on public approbation, however, is not primarily traceable to materialistic concerns. In the introductory remarks to his first reading
for his own profit the novelist specifically linked his
auditors with his readers, saying:

. . . I have had a pretty large experience of the interest my hearers are so generous as to take in these occasions, and of the delight they give to me, as a tried means of strengthening those relations—I may almost say of personal friendship—which it is my great privilege and pride, as it is my great responsibility, to hold with a multitude of persons who will never hear my voice nor see my face.

The confident tone of such remarks reflects the ready give-and-take between the writer and his public, built up over the years by the circumstances under which his novels were published. Thackeray, who also adopted the serial mode, observed that it promoted "communion between the writer and the public . . . something continual, confidential, something like personal affection." And Professors Butt and Tillotson in their important study, *Dickens at Work*, state: "Through serial publication an author could recover something of the intimate relationship between story-teller and audience which existed in the ages of the sagas and of Chaucer. . . ."

Readers, periodically renewing acquaintance with Dickens' characters over nineteen months, came to think of them as living people; and they did not hesitate to communicate to the author their hopes and fears over what future installments might hold in store. According to Forster, the painter David Wilkie made a speech at the banquet held to celebrate the completion of *Nicholas Nickleby* in which he praised "the reality of Dickens's genius," declaring

how there had been nothing like him issuing his novels part by part since Richardson issued his novels volume by volume, and how in both cases people talked about the characters as if they were next-door neighbours or friends, and how as many letters were written to the author of *Nickleby* to implore him not to kill poor Smike as had been sent by young ladies to the author of *Clarissa* to "save Lovelace's soul alive."

The death of Nell in *Old Curiosity Shop*, it is well known, became the occasion for widespread mourning. Sensing in advance that she was to die, a hoard of correspondents pled with the author to spare his heroine. Ruskin might cynically proclaim that "Nell was simply killed for the market, as a butcher kills a lamb"; but Dickens, who genuinely shared his audience's grief, was deeply gratified by the accumulating testimony that he had struck a common chord. In his first address after reaching Boston he dwelt on the enthusiastic American reception of his book. Despite their sentimentality, these remarks justify quotation at length for the light they throw on the kind of popular response which Dickens most valued:

I cannot help expressing the delight, the more than happiness it was to me to find so strong an interest awakened on this side of the water, in favour of that little heroine of mine, to whom your President has made allusion, who died in her youth. I had letters about that child, in England, from the dwellers in log-houses among the morasses and swamps, and densest forests, and deepest solitudes of the Far West. Many a sturdy hand, hard with the axe and spade, and browned by the summer's sun, has taken up the pen, and written to me a little history of domestic joy or sorrow, always coupled, I am proud to say, with something of interest in that little tale, or some comfort or happiness derived from it; and my correspondent has always addressed me, not as a writer of books for sale, resident some four or five thousand miles away, but as a friend to whom he might freely impart the joys and sorrows of his own fireside. Many a mother—I could reckon them now by dozens, not by units—has done the like, and has told me that she lost such a child at such a time, and where she is buried, and how good she was, and how, in this or that respect, she resembled Nell.

The novelist's tenderness for the sensibilities of his readers made him chary of causing gratuitous offense, even when some compromise of artistic purpose was required. The most notable example concerns the characterization of the dwarf Miss Mowcher, who is first presented in Chapter 22 of *David Copperfield* as a sinister procuress in Steerforth's employ. Dickens had modeled her on a deformed chiropodist, named Mrs. Hill; and when this person wrote in heartbroken protest against the apparent cruelty, Dickens altered his plan to show Miss Mowcher in a more sympathetic light. Similarly, he created the character of Riah in *Our Mutual Friend* in part to make amends for Fagin, after a Jewish acquaintance accused him of anti-Semitic bias.

Three times at least, Dickens, swayed by the representations of friends whose opinions he respected, made changes in his stories radically at odds with their initial design. When Lord Jeffrey, the eminent Scottish editor and critic and one of Dickens' warmest admirers, wrote expressing incredulity that Edith Dombey was Carkers' mistress, Dickens decided on the alternate relationship which he announced to Forster as follows: "What do you think of a kind of inverted Maid's Tragedy, and a tremendous scene of her undeceiving Carker, and giving him to know that she never meant that?" Forster himself took credit for having discouraged the author's notion of having Walter Gay in the same novel come to a bad end—a resolution then held over for Richard Carstone in *Bleak House*. With greater hesitation Dickens yielded to Bulwer Lytton's urging that the original ending of *Great Expectations*, in which Pip and Estella part forever after a final meeting, be changed to allow for the union of the chastened lovers. "I have put in as pretty a little piece of writing as I could," Forster was informed after the proofs had been revised, "and I have no doubt the story will be more acceptable through the alteration."

Yet, although critics have tended to explain away many of the elements in Dickens' art antipathetic to modern tastes on the grounds of the writer's too willing compliance with conventions in Victorian fiction, the examples which can be cited to show that Dickens went against his better judgment to satisfy the market demand are few in number. On the contrary, when his opinion of one of his works did not jibe with its contemporary reception, later generations of readers have almost invariably vindicated his own estimate. This has been the case with *Martin Chuzzlewit*, which continued to be lukewarmly received even after the introduction of the American episodes. Dickens wrote to Forster in 1843:

You know, as well as I, that I think Chuzzlewit in a hundred points immeasurably the best of my stories. That I feel my power now, more than I ever did. That I have a greater confidence in myself than I ever had. That I *know*, if I have health, I could sustain my place in the minds of thinking men, though fifty writers started up to-morrow. But how many readers do *not* think! How many take it upon trust from knaves and idiots, that one writes too fast, or runs a thing to death! How coldly did this very book go on for months, until it forced itself up in people's opinion, without forcing itself up in sale!

Gissing wisely insisted that "Dickens never conceives himself, when he aims at popularity, as writing *down* to his audience." This statement suggests the basis of the novelist's faith in his public. He perceived that the traditional system of aristocratic sponsorship, against which Samuel Johnson had rebelled, had been replaced by a new dispensation of corporate patronage. Now, thanks to the democratic revolution and the spread of education, the artist worked under the sufferance of the entire literate populace. Dickens' sense of the importance of this radical shift in responsibility is a recurrent theme in his addresses to literary and artistic groups; but he developed it most forcibly in a speech at Birmingham in 1853:

To the great compact phalanx of the people, by whose industry, perseverance, and intelligence, and their result in money-wealth such places as Birmingham, and many others like it, have arisen—to that great centre of support, that comprehensive experience, and that beating heart— Literature has turned happily from individual patrons, sometimes munificent, often sordid, always few, and has found there at once its highest purpose, its natural range of action, and its best reward. . . . From the shame of the purchased dedication, from the scurrilous and dirty work of Grub Street, from the dependent seat on sufferance at my Lord Duke's table today, and from the sponging-house and Marshalsea tomorrow, from that venality which, by a fine moral retribution, has degraded statesmen even to a greater extent than authors, because the statesmen entertained a low belief in the universality of corruption, while the author yielded only to the dire necessity of his calling,—from all such evils the people have set Literature free. And my creed in the exercise of that profession is, that Literature cannot be too faithful to the people in return—cannot too ardently advocate the cause of their advancement, happiness, and prosperity.

At all times unconcerned with the opinions of professional literary critics, Dickens resolved in 1838 to avoid reading reviews of his own writings. "What I had most indeed to notice in him at the very outset of his career," Forster said, "was his indifference to any praise of his performances on the merely literary side, compared with the higher recognition of them as bits of actual life, with the meaning and purpose on their part, and the responsibility on his, of realities rather than creatures of fancy." On the other hand,

Dickens' eagerness that his fiction be disseminated as widely as possible among the masses led in 1846 to plans for a "Cheap" edition to appear at weekly intervals in halfpenny numbers. The original Preface to this edition, subsequently discarded, was "dedicated to the English people, in whose approval, if the books be true in spirit, they will live, and out of whose memory, if they be false, they will very soon die."

Dickens was never content to think of himself merely as a popular entertainer; and he coupled enjoyment of success with a grave sense of the responsibilities entailed on a writer whose following numbered in the millions. The address to the reader in the first number of *Household Words* endorses with humble eloquence the conditions under which he held his sovereign position:

We have considered what an ambition it is to be admitted into many homes with affection and confidence; to be regarded as a friend by children and old people; to be thought of in affliction and in happiness; to people the sickroom with airy shapes "that give delight and hurt not," and to be associated with the harmless laughter and the gentle tears of many hearths. We know the great responsibility of such a privilege; its vast reward; the pictures that it conjures up, in hours of solitary labour, of a multitude moved by one sympathy; the solemn hopes which it awakens in the labourer's breast, that he may be free from self-reproach in looking back at last upon his work, and that his name may be remembered in his race in time to come, and borne by the dear objects of his love with pride. The hand that writes these faltering lines, happily associated with *some* Household Words before to-day, has known enough of such experiences to enter in an earnest spirit upon this new task, and with an awakened sense of all that it involves.

J. W. T. Ley, the editor of Forster's *Life*, is undoubtedly correct in ascribing the exculpatory state-

ment which Dickens published on separating from his
wife, to legitimate concern over the damage which
malicious rumors might inflict on the public image
which he had so carefully fostered. Ley writes:

It is true that he did value the peculiarly intimate relations that had always existed between him and his public,
and that he did always conscientiously hold that those
relations imposed upon him a moral responsibility. Anything which seemed to him even remotely to threaten
those good relations always gave rise to a sensitiveness
which was altogether worthy and above criticism.

Dickens embraced his position as one of the ac-
credited literary spokesmen of his age the more readily
because he did not find it in any way incommensurate
with artistic growth. From the outset of his career he
was never content to repeat his successes, so that it
may be said that, far from allowing the tastes of his
readers to determine his practice, he more than any
other writer of his time was instrumental in forming
those tastes. Even while *Pickwick Papers* was running
its merry course, *Oliver Twist* began to appear, serving notice that the audience which rejoiced in the
author's comic vein must also be prepared to share his
somber probings of the dark undersurface of Victorian society. The influential journals of the day
viewed the later novels with increasing asperity for a
variety of reasons: regret over the writer's failure to
cultivate the humorous and sentimental strains in his
early work; official resentment of his satiric onslaughts
on institutionalized evils; growing regard among sophisticated readers for the more deliberate artistry of
Thackeray and George Eliot. Yet, Dickens remained
a better judge of the temper of the general public
than his critics; and the great social novels of his
maturity, for which he is today preeminently admired,

enjoyed an unrivaled popularity in his own time, the sales of each successive story rising until at the time of his death the circulation of monthly parts of *The Mystery of Edwin Drood* had attained the unprecedented figure of fifty thousand.

FOUR
NARRATIVE ART

Every good actor plays direct to every good author, and every writer of fiction, though he may not adopt the dramatic form, writes in effect for the stage.

CHARLES DICKENS, SPEAKING AT DINNER FOR THE ROYAL GENERAL THEATRICAL FUND
—MARCH 29, 1858

What is exaggeration to one class of minds and perceptions, is plain truth to another. That which is commonly called a long-sight, perceives in prospect innumerable features and bearings non-existent to a short-sighted person. I sometimes ask myself whether there may occasionally be a difference of this kind between some writers and some readers; whether it is always the writer who colours highly, or whether it is now and then the reader whose eye for colour is a little dull?

Martin Chuzzlewit,
PREFACE

. . . I work slowly and with great care, and never give way to my invention recklessly, but constantly restrain it: and . . . I think it is my infirmity to fancy or perceive relations in things which are not apparent generally.

LETTER FROM CHARLES DICKENS TO SIR EDWARD BULWER LYTTON
—1865

 ICKENS WAS FIRST AND FOREMOST A STORYTELLER. IT WAS SO THAT HE THOUGHT OF HIMSELF; IT WAS SO THAT HE WAS RE-GARDED BY THE CONTEMPO-rary public for which, in the first instance, he wrote; and it is here that any critical examination of his achievement must begin. Like Shakespeare's plays, Dickens' novels are extraordinarily impure, in the sense that the writers of both were subject to many in-fluences and were wholly unpredictable in their ways of amalgamating these influences into works perfectly unique in their kind. Dickens' reading, although wider than is generally recognized, was undiscriminating. His novels assume familiarity with those great reposi-tories of English folk wisdom: the Bible; fairy tales, fables, and nursery rhymes; *The Pilgrim's Progress; Robinson Crusoe.* From his earliest years he had ac-cepted as mentors the eighteenth-century novelists and essayists, Smollett, Fielding, Sterne, Addison, Steele, and Goldsmith. His knowledge of the drama was en-cyclopedic, extending from Shakespeare, whom he had by heart, down to the pantomimes, burlesques, and extravaganzas, which formed the staples of the Vic-torian popular theater and to the love of which his writings constantly bear witness. In addition, he owes

a manifest debt to sources as disparate as the *Arabian Nights*, the Gothic romance, Scott, and Carlyle. Like Shakespeare again, however, what Dickens appropriated, he made so much his own that source studies are of limited validity in accounting for his artistic development. Nor was he ever much given to theorizing about his art. His correspondence and working notes relate, as a general rule, to the practical problems of planning the works in hand and accommodating them to the requirements of serialization.

Dickens' mastery over his medium is the record of his growth from a remarkably fecund improviser whose panoramic stories were presented as a series of discrete episodes to a writer capable of incorporating segments of narrative into complex, but tightly articulated, wholes. The conditions of publication in monthly or weekly installments discouraged, of course, unified plotting; and the two Prefaces to *Pickwick Papers*, the one for the first edition of 1837, the other for the "Cheap" edition of 1847, show awareness of this fact. The original Preface readily grants the episodic nature of the work for which he had contracted:

The author's object in this work, was to place before the reader a constant succession of characters and incidents; to paint them in as vivid colours as he could command; and to render them, at the same time, life-like and amusing.

When, however, Dickens refers back to this Preface a decade later, he does so on a note of apology. Admitting that "no ingenuity of plot was attempted, or even at that time considered very feasible by the author in connexion with the desultory mode of publication adopted," he goes on to confess, in the light of intervening "experience and study," that he "could perhaps wish now that these chapters were strung together on a stronger thread of general interest. . . ."

A letter to his early friend Thomas Mitton, written in 1839 while he was at work on *Nicholas Nickleby*, clearly shows the dilemma in which the writer found himself between the conception of each monthly part as a self-contained unit and broader concern for totality of effect:

I am doing the Snail at present—not the Railroad, and if I finish the next No. by next Saturday shall consider myself well off. The devil of it is, that I am afraid I must spoil a number now and then, for the sake of the book. It's a hard case, but I *ought* to be hard as iron to my own inclinations and do so.

The desire "to shorten the intervals of communication between himself and his readers," which led Dickens to embark in 1840 on *Master Humphrey's Clock*, did not at first seem incompatible with his artistic goals. The Preface expresses the intention: "In the execution of this weekly task, to have as much regard as its exigencies would permit, to each story as a whole, and to the possibility of its publication at some distant day, apart from the machinery in which it had its origin." The frustrations encountered in adapting *The Old Curiosity Shop* and *Barnaby Rudge* to weekly installments led, however, to second thoughts; and Dickens' announcement in October 1841 that he was discontinuing *Master Humphrey's Clock* is an important manifesto of his increasing preoccupation with narrative continuity:

I should not regard the anxiety, the close confinement, or the constant attention, inseparable from the weekly form of publication (for to commune with you in any form, is to me a labour of love), if I had found it advantageous to the conduct of my stories, the elucidation of my meaning, or the gradual development of my characters. But I have not done so. I have often felt cramped and confined in a very irksome and harassing degree, by the space in which I have been constrained to move. I have wanted you to know more at once than I could tell you; and it has frequently been of the greatest importance to my cherished intention, that you should do so. I have been sometimes strongly tempted (and have been at some pains to resist the temptation) to hurry incidents on, lest they should appear to you who waited from week to week, and had not, like me, the result and purpose in your minds, too long delayed. In a word, I have found this form of publication most anxious, perplexing, and difficult. I cannot bear these jerking confidences which are no sooner begun than ended, and no sooner ended than begun again.

Many passages in a tale of any length, depend materially for their interest on the intimate relation they bear to what has gone before, or to what is to follow. I sometimes found it difficult when I issued thirty-two closely-printed pages once a month, to sustain in your mind this needful connexion; in the present form of publication it is often, especially in the first half of a story, quite impossible to preserve it sufficiently through the current numbers. And although in my progress I am gradually able to set you right, and to show what my meaning has been, and to work it out, I see no reason why you should ever be wrong when I have it in my power, by resorting to a better means of communication between us, to prevent it.

The ensuing novel in monthly parts, *Martin Chuzzlewit*, was the first to be organized around a central theme, that of egoism. The resultant necessity for planning in advance had significant implications for the serial method, as the author acknowledged in his Preface to the completed work:

I have endeavoured in the progress of this Tale, to resist the temptation of the current Monthly Number, and to keep a steadier eye upon the general purpose and design.

With this object in view, I have put a strong constraint upon myself from time to time, in many places; and I hope the story is the better for it, now.

Henceforth the demands of overall form were to take priority over the balance and proportion of individual parts whenever the two came into conflict. The original Preface of *Little Dorrit*, for example, makes to the reader the following plea for suspended judgment:

I have been occupied with this story, during many working hours of two years. I must have been very ill employed, if I could not leave its merits and demerits as a whole, to express themselves on its being read as a whole. But, as it is not unreasonable to suppose that I may have held its various threads with a more continuous attention than anyone else can have given them during its desultory publication, it is not unreasonable to ask that the weaving may be looked at in its completed state, and with the pattern finished.

And the Postscript to *Our Mutual Friend* still more emphatically underscores the author's attention to unity of design:

To keep for a long time unsuspected, yet always working itself out, another purpose originating in that leading incident, and turning it to a pleasant and useful account at last, was at once the most interesting and the most difficult part of my design. Its difficulty was much enhanced by the mode of publication; for it would be very unreasonable to expect that many readers, pursuing a story in portions from month to month through nineteen months, will, until they have it before them complete, perceive the relations of its finer threads to the whole pattern which is always before the eyes of the story-weaver at his loom.

The vocabulary which Dickens habitually employs to describe his narrative methods is extremely reveal-

ing. In contrast to such novelists as Samuel Richardson
or Jane Austen or George Eliot or Henry James, he
never seeks even in his most mature work to create the
impression that his plots evolve by their own impetus
out of an inner logic of events. Form and meaning
do not organically coalesce; rather they are related
through a process of deliberate and overt manipulation.
To recur to Dickens' chosen analogy, the themes of
the later novels provide the warp or groundwork
through which the artist threads an intricate pattern
of interlocking episodes to impose the desired completeness and finality of design.

Dickens' fiction stems from the mingling of epic
and dramatic elements which imparted to the English
novel its characteristic form in the eighteenth century. Translated into prose narrative, the epic, beginning with Cervantes, issues in all the many varieties
of the picaresque tale. The novel's debt to drama is
equally manifest, whether in the broadly farcical scenes
of Fielding and Smollett or the obvious dependence of
the sensation novelists on stage melodrama. By temperament and experience Dickens was receptive to both
traditional strains. His life as a journalist prepared
him to emulate the great writers of the previous
century who ranged so broadly in recording the
spectacle of contemporary life, just as his passion for
the theater encouraged the tendency, in Ruskin's
phrase, "to speak in a circle of stage fire."

In popular narrative and dramatic modes, then,
Dickens found forms of expression conformable to his
imaginative vision; and he set out to perfect a manner
of his own through experimentation with their pos-
sibilities. The first six novels, from *Pickwick Papers* to
Martin Chuzzlewit, however original in substance, are
all more or less derivative in form, and exemplify the
writer's efforts to assimilate to his expanding purposes

literary fashions of proven appeal to the mass of
novel-readers and theater-goers.

Dickens' indebtedness to the fiction of Defoe,
Smollett, and Fielding is reflected in the titles of
many of his early stories, named after the heroes whose
careers they ostensibly set forth, as well as in the
elaborate and teasing chapter headings which occur as
late as *Dombey and Son*. Again, in the manner of the
picaresque tale, extensive portions of these works are
taken up with the protagonists' wanderings on jour-
neys that offer a constantly shifting kaleidoscope of
adventures, inviting every kind of treatment, whether
satiric, burlesque, sentimental, or pathetic. If Pickwick,
at least at the start, is the Quixotically lovable middle-
aged buffoon, Nicholas Nickleby and Martin Chuzzlewit represent bland versions of the youthful rogue.
And just as Pickwick has his Sancho Panza in Sam
Weller, so Nicholas and Martin are accompanied by
their youthful servitors, Smike and Mark Tapley.
Dickens even takes over from Cervantes and his fol-
lowers the device of interpolated tales to lend tonal
variety to *Pickwick Papers* and *Nicholas Nickleby*.

Because of its episodic nature the picaresque genre
can be adapted to a wide spectrum of subject matter.
Dickens notably extended its range to make room for
his love of the fabulous. This is particularly evident in
his use of motifs from folklore which add a fairy-tale
dimension to so many of his novels. A related aspect of
the writer's practice evokes an allegorical or exemplary
frame of reference. The original title, *Oliver Twist,
or, the Parish Boy's Progress,* indicates the author's
debt to Bunyan in that work. Introducing Nell to the
reader, Master Humphrey remarks that "she seemed to
exist in a kind of allegory," and her wayfaring is several
times likened to a pilgrimage.

The dissatisfaction which Dickens early felt with

the random and inconsecutive nature of the picaresque manner is apparent, however, from his efforts to give his stories greater cohesiveness. The nine intercalated tales in *Pickwick Papers* are so placed as to provide a somber commentary on the leading episodes in the main action; and all readers have observed that Pickwick's imprisonment in the Fleet signalizes a notable tightening of narrative control. In *Nicholas Nickleby*, which includes only two incidental tales, a counterpointing effect is achieved through the double story line, the hero's exploits being with some consistency played off against his sister's misadventures. In *The Old Curiosity Shop* the author was clearly endeavoring to combine the narrative sweep of *Pickwick Papers* with the denser atmospheric unity of *Oliver Twist;* and while there is still a want of tonal consistency, a measure of continuity accrues from the author's use of the chase to create suspense, as Nell flies from the city to escape Quilp. In his choice of an historical setting for *Barnaby Rudge*, Dickens was, at least in part, motivated by the desire to rival Scott; and the example of the earlier novelist was beneficial to the extent that the Gordon Riots provided occasion for a sustained display of descriptive virtuosity unparalleled in the writer's previous work. With *Martin Chuzzlewit*, finally, Dickens discovered how to hold in tension the diverse elements of a many-faceted story by associating them with a single theme. Bondage to self unites narrative strands as divergent as Martin's deluded excursion to the United States, Pecksniff's hypocritical dodges, Tigg's bold-faced chicanery, and Mrs. Gamp's histrionic antics.

Like Fielding's, Dickens' manner is primarily scenic, originating in a sure feeling for theatrical effects. The opening of Chapter 17 of *Oliver Twist* succinctly summarizes the characteristics of contemporary melo-drama. The passage begins:

It is the custom on the stage, in all good murderous melo-dramas, to present the tragic and comic scenes, in as regular alternation, as the layers of red and white in a side of streaky bacon. The hero sinks upon his straw bed, weighed down by fetters and misfortunes; in the next scene, his faithful but unconscious squire regales the audience with a comic song. We behold, with throbbing bosoms, the heroine in the grasp of a proud and ruthless baron: her virtue and her life alike in danger, drawing forth her dagger to preserve the one at the cost of the other; and just as our expectations are wrought up to the highest pitch, a whistle is heard, and we are straightway transported to the great hall of the castle: where a grey-headed seneschal sings a funny chorus with a funnier body of vassals, who are free of all sorts of places, from church vaults to palaces, and roam about in company, carolling perpetually.

The ensuing paragraph goes on to suggest that these abrupt changes are more in the habitual course of things than living actors on the stage of life are apt to realize:

Such changes appear absurd; but they are not so un-natural as they would seem at first sight. The transitions in real life from well-spread boards to death-beds, and from mourning-weeds to holiday garments, are not a whit less startling; only, there, we are busy actors, instead of passive lookers-on, which makes a vast difference. The actors in the mimic life of the theatre, are blind to violent transitions and abrupt impulses of passion or feeling, which, presented before the eyes of mere spectators, are at once condemned as outrageous and preposterous.

The early novels are remarkable for individual scenes; and the fact that this is so is owing to their dramatic conception. Oliver in the poorhouse asking for a second helping of gruel and the death of Sikes linger in memory after all the contrivances on which the plot of *Oliver Twist* hinges have gone out of mind. The "streaky bacon" alternations to which Dickens refers are exemplified in the opening of *Nicholas Nickleby* where, by the most abrupt of transitions, the hero moves from Dotheboys Hall to Vincent Crummles' strolling troupe. Of Dickens' genius for hilariously comic episodes it is hardly necessary to speak. Every reader will have his own favorites: the trial in *Pickwick Papers*, Mrs. Nickleby's wooing by "the gentleman next door," Pecksniff's drunken frolic at Todgers's. But the primary importance of scene as a structural unit in Dickens' early fiction is still better illustrated by the great passages of melodramatic action to which the stories build through mounting suspense.

Dickens was fascinated by violence from childhood, when his nurse fed his imagination with blood-curdling yarns. He told Forster of the avidity with which later during schooldays he devoured "penny dreadfuls":

I used, when I was at school, to take in the *Terrific Register*, making myself unspeakably miserable, and frightening my very wits out of my head, for the small charge of a penny weekly; which considering that there was an illustration to every number, in which there was always a pool of blood, and at least one body, was cheap.

And Edmund Wilson in his psychoanalytic discussion of Dickens' writings discerns in the macabre tales in *Pickwick Papers* early evidence of the novelist's life-long obsession with the workings of the criminal mind. It may be that this side of Dickens' nature speaks with special cogency to the lawless and unprincipled modern world which has shown a disposition to accept the prevalence of bloodshed and cruelty in these novels, while rejecting everything that smacks of sentimentality or pathos. However this may be, there can be no disputing the absolute scenic mastery demonstrated in many of the great set pieces of the early novels: the death of Sikes, Jonas Chuzzlewit's murder of Tigg, the burning of the Warren and of Newgate in *Barnaby Rudge.*

In calling on the conventional artifices of melodramatic plotting, Dickens was endeavoring to replace the straight linear progression of the picaresque tale with a more involved type of narrative, as a comparison of *Oliver Twist* with *Pickwick Papers* makes clear. Nevertheless, no amount of stage machinery can disguise the absence of organic structure in the early stories. Dickens' second novel originates in the declared purpose "to show the principle of Good surviving through every adverse circumstance." Oliver is the first embodiment of a conception to which his creator was to return more than once—the lost child; and the sequence of episodes which subjects the helpless boy to one malignant environment after another could hardly be bettered. The eventual working out of his fortunes is, however, outrageously fabricated. Monks' villainy, with the accompanying business of hidden identities, concealed relationships, and destroyed wills, illustrates every excess of the sensation novel; and the counteracting forces of good, vested in Mr. Brownlow and the Maylies, operate in an equally preposterous way. A similar theme inspired *The Old Curiosity Shop,* in the Preface to which the author states:

. . . in writing the book, I had it always in my fancy to surround the lonely figure of the child with grotesque and wild, but not impossible, companions, and to gather about

her innocent face and pure intentions, associates as strange
and uncongenial as the grim objects that are about her
bed when her history is first foreshadowed.

Here again the stark black and white division of the
moral world between the contending forces of vice and
virtue falsifies Nell's ordeal. Quilp's monstrous hound-
ing of the heroine seems largely gratuitous, and save
for excruciating the reader's emotions, it is difficult to
see what purpose is served by her death. Although
in *Barnaby Rudge* sons are uniformly victimized by
their fathers, the pattern of parental oppression so
central to Dickens' later themes has no radical connection with the development of the story.

Oliver and Nell and Barnaby are passive under
their misfortunes. They are the occasion for good or
evil actions by others, but do not themselves initiate
any significant developments in their respective stories.
Nicholas Nickleby and Martin Chuzzlewit are equally
vapid—colorless transcriptions of the picaresque pro-
totype. Nicholas is, by and large, the author's agent
for passing in review various conditions of contemporary life about which he was moved to write. Ralph
Nickleby's plot to betray Kate to Sir Mulberry Hawk,
which only tangentially involves Nicholas, is a stock
situation to create additional suspense, and the same is
true of the tawdry intrigue relating to Madeline and
Gride. In this novel more than any other the reader
senses a lack of narrative direction. Through long sec-
tions the author is simply applying the familiar formula
for melodrama: "Make 'em laugh; make 'em cry; make
'em wait."

The incidents in *Martin Chuzzlewit* are more
closely linked by the encompassing theme. Young
Martin's hardships in America, for example, instill in
him a new regard to the well-being of others. The role

of the protagonist, however, is peripheral to nearly
all of the striking scenes. Indeed, remarking on the
novel's Jonsonian ground plan, Forster writes that "the
notion of taking Pecksniff for a type of character was
really the origin of the book; the design being to
show, more or less by every person introduced, the
number and variety of humours and vices that have
their root in selfishness." And finally, *Barnaby Rudge*
sets up two discrete stories, since the lurid murder
mystery adumbrated in the first half has no real bearing on the spectacular treatment of the mob scenes
which follow.

Before leaving the subject, something should be
said about the relationship between Dickens' fictional
practices and the popular dramatic entertainments of
the day. The middle-class audience which crowded
into the vast Victorian theaters was the same public
that eagerly awaited the numbers of *Nicholas Nickleby*
and *The Old Curiosity Shop;* and the problems of communication across the footlights or by the printed
word were in many respects the same. For the motley
offerings of the pantomimes, burlesques, extravaganzas,
and melodramas which captured the fancy of contemporary theater-goers, Dickens substituted the
equally varied fare of his packed installments. And just
as writers for the stage used stock characters and situations, bold contrasts of mood ranging from buffoonery
to pathos and horror, broadly stylized mannerisms of
gesture and speech, and elaborate settings and tricks
of stagecraft, so Dickens exploited their counterparts
in his stories. Since each section of narrative must make
an immediate impact, like a self-contained but tonally
diversified skit, but since there was as well the necessity
of sustaining interest from week to week or month to
month, he appropriated from the stage a vast repertory
of artifices to create expectation of what was to come

and to facilitate the retention of what had already taken place. To his reliance on the familiar intrigues of farce and melodrama with their parallel situations and duplicating episodes should be added such additional devices, more particularly associated with characterization, as tag lines, eccentricities of dress and manner, and the display of conventionalized affectations, all designed to promote the reader's continuing involvement in the story.

In summary, the first decade of Dickens' literary career, during which he wrote six novels, was a period of constant experimentation, when he explored his narrative talents under the influence of prevalent modes in fiction and the drama. He had yet to achieve the consistency of attitude toward his material which would enable him to coordinate his storytelling skills in unified imaginative creations. This all-important stage in his development came during the 1840s with the deepening of his social consciousness, brought about in part by participation in public life, but inspired as well by the contagious zeal of such reformers as Carlyle. *Dombey and Son* is the first of Dickens' novels to project a unitary view of society in terms of class structure. The relevance of this view to the novelist's social criticism has been often remarked; but less attention has been paid to its artistic implications, particularly as affecting the organization of his narratives.

Dombey and Son, like its predecessors, has the breadth of focus that was the heritage of the picaresque tradition; but here the action is more purposefully controlled by its setting amidst the conditions of contemporary life. The theme is pride, as egoism was of *Martin Chuzzlewit*; but whereas in the previous work the governing vice is largely divorced from historical context, Dombey's pride is an inseparable component

of his mentality as a representative of the commercial
middle class. Contrary to his usual practice, Dickens
outlined to Forster his plans for the new novel. This
passage provides unmistakable evidence that the writer
had come to feel the need for working out his story
in advance, and also indicates his progress toward a
more organic concept of plot structure:

I design to show Mr. D. with that one idea of the Son taking firmer and firmer possession of him, and swelling and
bloating his pride to a prodigious extent. As the boy begins
to grow up, I shall show him quite impatient for his getting
on, and urging his masters to set him great tasks, and the
like. But the natural affection of the boy will turn to the
despised sister; and I purpose showing her learning all sorts
of things, of her own application and determination, to
assist him in his lessons: and helping him always. When
the boy is about ten years old (in the fourth number), he
will be taken ill, and will die; and when he is ill, and
when he is dying, I mean to make him turn always for
refuge to the sister still, and keep the stern affection of
the father at a distance. So Mr. Dombey—for all his
greatness, and for all his devotion to the child—will find
himself at arms' length from him even then; and will see
that his love and confidence are all bestowed upon his
sister, whom Mr. Dombey has used—and so has the boy
himself too, for that matter—as a mere convenience and
handle to him. The death of the boy is a death-blow, of
course, to all the father's schemes and cherished hopes;
and "Dombey and Son," as Miss Tox will say at the end
of the number, "is a Daughter after all." . . . From that
time, I purpose changing his feeling of indifference and
uneasiness towards his daughter into a positive hatred. For
he will always remember how the boy had his arm round
her neck when he was dying, and whispered to her, and
would take things only from her hand, and never thought
of him. . . . At the same time I shall change *her* feeling
towards him for one of a greater desire to love him, and
to be loved by him; engendered in her compassion for
his loss, and her love for the dead boy whom, in his way,
he loved so well too. So I mean to carry the story on,

through all the branches and off-shoots and meanderings that come up; and through the decay and downfall of the house, and the bankruptcy of Dombey, and all the rest of it; when his only staff and treasure, and his unknown Good Genius always, will be this rejected daughter, who will come out better than any son at last, and whose love for him, when discovered and understood, will be his bitterest reproach. For the struggle with himself, which goes on in all such obstinate natures, will have ended then; and the sense of his injustice, which you may be sure has never quitted him, will have at last a gentler office than of only making him more harshly unjust. . . . I rely very much on Susan Nipper grown up, and acting partly as Florence's maid, and partly as a kind of companion to her, for a strong character throughout the book. I also rely on the Toodles, and on Polly, who like everybody else, will be found by Mr. Dombey to have gone over to his daughter and become attached to her. This is what cooks call "the stock of the soup." All kinds of things will be added to it, of course.

The foregoing summary, it will be noted, includes no reference to Dombey's second marriage, or to Carker's role in the downfall of his fortunes; but these later developments are a natural enough outgrowth of the initial design. The same aggressive and coldly materialistic class-consciousness, which leads Dombey systematically to destroy his children's lives, carries over to his calculated cheapening of the marriage bond. That the two motifs were from the outset connected in the author's mind is apparent from Hablot Browne's cover design, which Dickens referred to as "shadowing out [the] drift and bearing" of his novel.

In his recipe for what he called "the stock of the soup," Dickens announced that "all kinds of things would be added"; and reporting progress to Forster he jubilantly stated: "I think *Dombey* very strong—with great capacity in its leading idea; plenty of character that is likely to tell; and some rollicking facetiousness, to say nothing of pathos." In other words, the author did not find increasing care for total design incommensurate with the demands of the individual parts. Although some memoranda for *The Old Curiosity Shop* and for two issues of *Martin Chuzzlewit* survive, *Dombey and Son* is apparently the first novel for which Dickens consistently prepared working notes, as was to be his habit for all subsequent works except *A Tale of Two Cities* and *Great Expectations*. These number plans, indispensable for the study of Dickens' authorial habits in the later stages of his career, are described in *Dickens at Work* by Professors Butt and Tillotson, and in *Dickens Romancier* by Professor Sylvère Monod. Of their general purpose the authors of the former volume have written:

These were the kind of notes which experience showed that his system of publication and his manner of work required of him. They do not determine the pattern of the novel, they do not define the path of the story, but they ensure that, the pattern once determined, the threads do not go awry, and, the path once set, there is no serious deviation in a course of as much as nineteen months. Furthermore, they have an abiding interest in that they shed light on the design in the pattern and serve to show the measure of control which Dickens exercised.

Dickens followed a uniform procedure in his notations for works in progress. They were entered on the facing halves of a folded sheet of paper. The right-hand side, serving what has been called "the recording function," usually contains a chapter-by-chapter summary of the principal episodes of the installment. The left-hand space, reserved for "the planning function," sheds much more light on the creative process itself. Here the author deliberates over a large variety of practical considerations with regard to the handling of

his story. The jottings include catch phrases and hints
for motifs still to be developed, trial versions of characters' names and directions for their entrances and
exits, speculations about the placing and structuring of
incidents. Frequently the memoranda take the form
of self-queries, as the writer debates the immediate
use, postponement, or rejection of material, alternate
ways of presenting it, questions of emphasis and tone.

The evidence provided by the number plans that
Dickens was learning to make each strand in his stories
contributory to the total design is corroborated by his
treatment of the two most sensational happenings in
Dombey and Son, the deaths of Paul Dombey and
Carker. Mrs. Dombey's demise in the first chapter fore-
shadows and sets the stage for that of Paul. Not only
does the dying mother turn from her husband to her
daughter for final consolation, but the moment of
death introduces the metaphor of mutability which
dominates Paul's dying fancies: "Thus, clinging fast
to that slight spar within her arms, the mother drifted
out upon the dark and unknown sea that rolls round
all the world." The notes for Chapter 14 state: "Paul's
illness only expressed in the child's own feelings. News
of Paul's illness. No. Not otherwise described." Dickens
thus compels the reader to identify himself with the
boy's own point of view as his life flows away. This
technique, combined with the obvious centrality of the
event in the unfolding plot, relieves the passage of
much of the sentimental irrelevance of Nell's death.
Carker's melodramatic end goes far to atone for the
egregiously stilted encounter between him and Edith
Dombey at Dijon, which was, as has been said, an
afterthought on the author's part. From early in the
story the railway has been established as a second and
more violent image of change; and indeed, in Chapter
20, describing Dombey's dreary rail journey to Leam-

ington, it is explicitly apostrophized as "the remorse-less monster, Death." There is, then, perfect dramatic appropriateness in its evocation as the nemesis on which Carker rushes, the more so since the reader accompanies that character on his baffled flight, subjectively sharing the accelerating impressions that anticipate the catastrophe.

Dickens' choice of first-person narrative for his next novel, *David Copperfield*, may have been in part influenced, as has been said, by Charlotte Brontë's brilliant success with the same mode in *Jane Eyre* the preceding year. Both stories trace the stages leading to the protagonists' discovery of their true identities; and Jane and David undergo similar ordeals entailing loss of innocence through revolt against injustice and banishment from their homes. By consistently assuming his hero's point of view Dickens is able to impart a new element of psychological continuity to the picaresque form, indeed to invest it with the continuity of the *Bildungsroman*. An early critic in the *Perspective Review* (1851) acutely remarked of *David Copperfield*:

by the adoption of this difficult form of writing the author has secured a unity and completeness which we have never seen equalled in a serial tale. It is in truth a very fine specimen of constructive skill. Complicated as the story is, and numerous as are the characters, all flows naturally from the mouth of the narrator, never leaving us to wonder how he got his information, and scarcely ever encumbered with devices to supply the gaps in his personal knowledge. Wonderfully well has the author succeeded in identifying himself with his principal personage. Every line is coloured with the hues of memory, and the subdued tone of a distant view is given to the whole. . . .

In addition, "the blending of experience and imagination," which David says is inseparable from the act of remembering, introduces a still more comprehensive unity of the order of myth. For all their vivid actuality, David's recollections of his childhood at Blunderstone Rookery, of his visits to Peggotty's boathouse, of his flight to Betsey Trotwood, of his schooldays at Rochester, and of his marriage to Dora create an aura of fantasy akin to the fairy-tale world with which these passages are so constantly associated. To achieve this atmospheric consistency Dickens subtly manipulates the time sequence to produce a kind of double focus. The reader is at once with the experiencing youth (note, for example, the four retrospective chapters told in the present tense) and with the mature man who assesses the meaning of these experiences. As the gap between past and present closes, the life pattern assumes coherence. It is not until Chapter 45, and even then only through vicarious involvement in the Strongs' marital affairs, that David becomes aware of the need to discipline the heart's impulses and so arrives at full self-knowledge.

Steerforth's role in *David Copperfield* posed the additional problem of reconciling two separate stories. In contrast to the relationships which directly affect David's growth to maturity, the portions of the tale treating Em'ly's seduction and its aftermath lack conviction. A number of scenes (of which the confrontation between Em'ly and Rosa Dartle is the most obtrusive example) are in the worst melodramatic manner of the early novels, since they attempt to coerce sympathy on grounds that have been insufficiently prepared. There are indications, however, that Dickens was beginning to work his way toward the kind of plot, later to be perfected, in which the action itself would become the principal means of elucidating theme. The sea, invoked metaphorically in *Dombey and Son* to foretell Paul's death, is translated in *David*

Copperfield into the agent of retributive justice. As Peggotty prepares to set out in search of Em'ly, a significant exchange takes place between David and Ham. The latter has fallen into a reverie; and when David asks what he is thinking about, the mariner replies:

"On what's afore me, Mas'r Davy; and over yon."

"On the life before you, do you mean?" He had pointed confusedly out to sea.

"Ay, Mas'r Davy. I doen't rightly know how 'tis, but from over yon there seemed to me to come—the end of it like;" looking at me as if he were waking, but with the same determined face.

"What end?" I asked, possessed by my former fear.

"I doen't know," he said thoughtfully. "I was calling to mind that the beginning of it all did take place here—and then the end come. . . ."

"The remembrance of this . . . ," David adds, "haunted me at intervals, even until the inexorable end came at its appointed time." Steerforth's death in the grand storm scene in Chapter 55 thus seems in no sense coincidental, but rather the terminal link in a predestined chain of cause and effect. Furthermore, the narrator's memories have been ironically ordered to forecast this denouement. The concluding paragraphs of Chapters 6 and 29 present David's view of Steerforth in precisely the posture, head on arm, in which the waves leave his drowned body on the beach at Yarmouth.

Bleak House is in many ways the masterpiece of Dickens' narrative art. For this novel the author undertook to fuse the methods of *Dombey and Son* and *David Copperfield*. The all-pervasive evil emanating from the legal case of Jarndyce and Jarndyce is objectively presented by an impersonal narrator. The blighting influence of this evil on the individual lives involved in the case is rendered in the first-person account of Esther Summerson. Of the 67 chapters, 33 or almost exactly half are given to Esther, while the omniscient speaker reserves the remaining 34 for himself. So skillfully are the two points of view spliced that they occur in alternation in fourteen of the twenty monthly parts. Only one installment is wholly devoted to Esther's narrative, and five to that of the commentator.

The omniscient voice speaks in the present tense. The dramatic potentialities of this mode Dickens exploits with extraordinary mastery in such chapters as that describing Captain Hawdon's death, where the reader, unaware of what lies in store, proceeds through accumulating suspense to the horrible revelation. Scenes are discontinuous, spatially related in shifting patterns that create a kaleidoscopic effect. The action advances by a process of episodic intensification. Thus, Chapter 31, in which Esther is smitten with smallpox, is immediately followed by the description of Krook's incineration; and Jo's pathetic death and Tulkinghorn's murder occur in successive chapters. Both pairs of dramatic events take place within single installments, furthermore, so that the full impact aimed at in juxtaposing these climactic scenes came across to the original readers.

Bleak House is the first of Dickens' novels to postulate a completely organic view of society. The arrangement of episodes reinforces in narrative terms the impression of interconnectedness accruing from the web of character relationships and the points of identity between the various settings. It has been objected that too much of the action is fortuitous. Gissing, for example, wrote:

In the fable of *Bleak House* there is much ingenuity, but an almost total disregard of probability; the fitting of incidents suggests a mechanical puzzle rather than the complications of human life; arbitrary coincidence takes the place of well-contrived motive, and at times the motive suggested is glaringly inadequate.

Yet, where so much is accidental, the reader's normal concern for verisimilitude is suspended. Dickens, indeed, viewed the world as a place where individual destinies constantly intersect under the inscrutable dispensations of chance. Forster states that the writer often spoke of "his favourite theory as to the smallness of the world, and how things and persons apparently the most unlikely to meet were continually knocking up against each other." And in another place Dickens' biographer remarks:

On the coincidences, resemblances, and surprises of life Dickens liked especially to dwell, and few things moved his fancy so pleasantly. The world, he would say, was so much smaller than we thought it; we were all so connected by fate without knowing it; people supposed to be far apart were so constantly elbowing each other; and tomorrow bore so close a resemblance to nothing half so much as yesterday.

In Dickens' world, however, the apparent randomness of existence conceals an underlying providence. Although the earlier novels frequently hint at this belief, it was as yet unembodied in credible actions. "How all things come about!" cries Monks when he is unmasked; and Dickens comments in *Martin Chuzzlewit* on "the remorseless course" of the history which he is unfolding. Not before *Bleak House*, however, does the writer succeed in creating a machinery of events so intermeshed that it needs only to be set in motion to operate with something of the inevitability of fate in classical drama.

Of the plotting of *Bleak House* Forster, who so

often anticipates the findings of later critics, has this to say:

Nothing is introduced at random, everything tends to the catastrophe, the various lines of the plot converge and fit to its centre, and to the larger interest all the rest is irresistibly drawn. The heart of the story is a Chancery suit. On this the plot hinges; and on incidents connected with it, trivial or important, the passion and suffering turn exclusively. Chance words, or the deeds of chance people, to appearance irrelevant, are found everywhere influencing the course taken by a train of incidents of which the issue is life or death, happiness or misery, to men and women perfectly unknown to them, and to whom they are unknown.

The aptness of this judgment could be substantiated by innumerable episodes in the novel; but two, bearing on the exposure of Lady Dedlock's guilt, will suffice for illustrative purposes. The chase, proverbially one of the surest devices for building suspense, has rarely been employed more adeptly than in *Bleak House*. Alerted by different clues, coincidentally discovered, and motivated by wholly different aims, Guppy and Tulkinghorn are unwittingly pitted against each other on the trail of the unhappy woman. On the verge of discovery Lady Dedlock is saved from each of her persecutors by the intervention of violent death, first Krook's, then Tulkinghorn's. But the pursuit is immediately taken over by Bucket and Esther who follow her to her own death. A different train of circumstances unites Lady Dedlock's fate with two beings at the very farthest remove from her in the social scale—Jo, the despised crossing-sweeper, and Jenny, the brickmaker's wife. In the workings of the plot these characters become the agents of a transcendent moral purpose which dooms those who deny the sacred impulses of the heart. For Jo and Jenny had been kindly treated by Captain Hawdon and Esther, the lover and child whom Lady Dedlock has rejected.

In contrast to the concept of an inexorably stern providence, Esther through her narrative represents the presence of loving compassion imminent in the human spirit. Whereas Dickens as omniscient recorder savagely excoriates social oppression, Esther speaking in her own person voices a counterbalancing sympathy with the victims of all such oppression. Since she is looking back on events that occurred seven years before, her recollections oppose a temporal dimension to the spatial pattern of dovetailing episodes in the historical present. Happenings which seem discontinuous and coincidental when viewed objectively offer in Esther's perspective the appearance of a sequential and causally ordered progression. As she remarks with reference to Ada's mute suffering over Richard's involvement in Chancery proceedings: ". . . I observed it in many slight particulars which were nothing in themselves and only became something when they were pieced together." Early in the story John Jarndyce admonishes Richard: "Trust in nothing but Providence and your own efforts. Never separate the two. . . ." Although one may take exception to Esther's saccharine naïveté, so typical of Dickens' girl heroines, it is her cooperant will which infuses the redemptive power of love into the wasteland of *Bleak House*, as Charley and Jenny, Caddy Jellyby and Ada Clare are present to attest.

Admittedly something of a *tour de force* in its split narrative technique, *Bleak House* heralds further experimentation with methods of shaping and integrating the multifarious materials of Dickens' fiction into harmonious wholes. The slips on which the author wrote the periodic installments of his stories reveal that by the time of *Martin Chuzzlewit* he no longer trusted the improvisatorial facility of the early years and that the act of composition was becoming an altogether more laborious business. Hereafter, each successive manuscript, together with the number plans, bears evidences of the increasingly stringent artistic demands which Dickens made on himself. Of *Our Mutual Friend*, his last complete work, he wrote to Forster: "I have grown hard to satisfy, and write very slowly." The change is graphically illustrated by two facsimiles reproduced in Forster's *Life*, the one of a slip from *Oliver Twist* sent to the printer almost without revision, the other of the final completed page of *The Mystery of Edwin Drood*, so heavily scored over and interlineated as to be almost illegible.

The biography also gives telltale listings of the various titles for his books which Dickens mulled over from *David Copperfield* on. He found it difficult to embark on a new story until he had decided what it was to be called; and the alternate names, suggestive of different approaches and emphases, clearly indicate that this hesitation resulted from the need to have a clear plan in mind. In making memoranda for the second number of *Hard Times*, Dickens concluded that the action of this novel logically fell into three divisions, which were entitled "Sowing," "Reaping," and "Garnering" when the work was published in its entirety. All subsequent novels were mapped out in books or parts; and a statement about *Great Expectations* shows that Dickens had come to regard these structural units as integral to the total design: "It is a pity that the third portion cannot be read all at once, because its purpose would be much more apparent; and the pity is the greater, because the general turn and tone of the working out and winding up, will be away from all such things as they conventionally go."

In contrast to earlier works, the opening scenes

of the later novels exhibit a confident artistry, further indicative of scrupulous forethought. They not only announce leading themes for subsequent development, but also immediately and dramatically enlist the reader's interest in series of events, the resolution of which may be withheld for many hundreds of pages. Especially noteworthy is the first chapter of *Our Mutual Friend*, which presents Lizzie Hexam rowing her father along the Thames in pursuit of his ghastly traffic in drowned corpses. The girl's obvious repugnance to his calling draws from Gaffer the following complaint:

"How can you be so thankless to your best friend, Lizzie? The very fire that warmed you when you were a baby, was picked out of the river alongside the coal barges. The very basket that you slept in, the tide washed ashore. The very rockers that I put it upon to make a cradle of it, I cut out of a piece of wood that drifted from some ship or another."

But Lizzie will have better reasons for being grateful for her early apprenticeship to the Thames; for the skill in boat-handling then acquired enables her at the climax of the story to retrieve Eugene's battered body from its waters. Dickens' notes for this episode in the seventeenth number read: "Back to the opening chapter. *Strongly*."

A clearer notion of the increasingly rigorous control which Dickens exercised over his materials may be gained by briefly considering two pairs of novels which offer grounds for comparison. *A Tale of Two Cities*, like *Barnaby Rudge*, resorts to an historical setting; but in the earlier book the writer had not yet learned how to project the private lives of his characters against a background of public events. The mob violence, released by the Gordon Riots of 1780, although late in erupting, develops such torrential force, thanks to Dickens' descriptive power, that it ends by overflowing and obscuring the contours of the framing narrative. The French Revolution, on the other hand, is from the start the focal center of *A Tale of Two Cities*; all elements of the story are gradually, but inevitably magnetized by it. A letter to Forster in 1859 leaves no doubt that in this novel Dickens concentrated his attention more fully than ever before on unity of action:

. . . I set myself the little task of making *a picturesque story*, rising in every chapter, with characters true to nature, but whom the story itself should express, more than they should express themselves, by dialogue. I mean, in other words, that I fancied a story of incident might be written, in place of the odious stuff that *is* written under that pretence, pounding the characters out in its own mortar, and beating their interests out of them. If you could have read the story all at once, I hope you wouldn't have stopped halfway.

When Wilkie Collins objected that the reader had not been sufficiently prepared for Charles Darnay's fate, Dickens replied: "I think the business of art is to lay all the ground carefully, not with the care that conceals itself—to show, by a backward light, what everything has been working to—but only to *suggest*, until the fulfilment comes. These are the ways of Providence, of which all art is but a little imitation." Equally significant is the argument with which the novelist met Forster's criticism that Madame Defarge's death at the hands of Miss Pross is not sufficiently credible:

I am not clear, and I never have been, respecting the canon of fiction which forbids the interposition of accident in such a case as Madame Defarge's death. Where the accident is inseparable from the passion and action of the character; where it is strictly consistent with the entire design, and arises out of some culminating proceeding on the part of the individual which the whole story has led up to; it seems to me to become, as it were, an act of divine justice. And when I use Miss Pross . . . to bring about such a catastrophe, I have the positive intention of making that half-comic intervention a part of the desperate woman's failure; and of opposing that mean death, instead of a desperate one in the streets which she wouldn't have minded, to the dignity of Carton's. Wrong or right, this was all design, and seemed to me to be in the fitness of things.

The role of Miss Pross is the culminating example of a type of resolution occurring in many of Dickens' novels. The power of evil is formidably strong in his, as in Shakespeare's, world; and the novelist's villains, like those of the dramatist, are as a general rule not only more intelligent, but also stronger willed than their adversaries. Through their resourcefulness and egoism they exert kinds of power which disarm the forces of good. Frequently, as in Shakespearean tragedy, they are entrapped in their machinations and bring about their own downfall; but more often they are defeated by minor and apparently ineffectual characters in scenes that recall the traditionally comic device of unmasking. This peculiarly Dickensian form of poetic justice leads to a number of unpredictable, but conclusive showdowns between characters as ill-assorted as Micawber and Uriah Heep, Sissy Jupe and James Harthouse, and Pancks and Casby.

For *Great Expectations* Dickens returned to the autobiographical mode of *David Copperfield*; but Pip is far more the protagonist of his story than David of his. There is no scene in which Pip does not play an instrumental part, whereas, after the opening chapters of the earlier novel, David is reduced to the role of passive onlooker at the rival complications involving Uriah and the Wickfields, Steerforth and the Peggottys, Jack Malden and the Strongs. Even the great childhood scenes lack the immediacy of their counterparts in *Great Expectations*. David's reconstruction of his early years has the quality of "emotion recollected in tranquillity"; the prevailing tone of nostalgic regret for lost innocence produces an impression of remoteness, relegating the speaker's experiences to an idyllic past. In *Great Expectations* the reader is at once immersed in the boy's subjective responses, as Pip seeks to establish his identity *vis-à-vis* the imperfectly understood world which is opening up around him. Dickens' method of limiting point of view is cinematographic, varying in the opening chapter from the close-up when Magwitch first erupts on Pip's terrified vision to the long shot of the criminal's departure over the marshes, which conveys a first intimation of furtive sympathy. Pip's physical upending by Magwitch in the graveyard has its moral analogue in a dislocation of values, not to be restored to equilibrium until the hero learns to distinguish between appearance and reality, both in his own being and in his relations with others. For Pip's expectations are erected on a basis of ironic misconceptions. Miss Havisham, the putative fairy godmother, turns out to be the evil witch; Magwitch is transmuted from villain into surrogate parent and would-be benefactor, replacing the rejected Joe; Estella, far from being the princess of the tale, is revealed as Magwitch's true child by a murderess.

David stumbles on the truth about himself through the examples of others; Pip slowly and painfully acquires self-knowledge by learning to accept responsibility for his own actions. Although he is slow to piece them together, the clues by which, in Pip's own phraseology, he is to be followed into his "poor labyrinth" are so artfully disposed by the author that each episode only becomes fully meaningful in the light of all that has come before and will follow after. Thus, to take only one example, Pip's sense of complicity with lawbreakers grows out of his theft for Magwitch. The leg manacle, severed by the stolen file, provides the weapon with which Orlick bludgeons Mrs. Gargery; and this deed prepares in turn for the great scene at the lime kiln when Pip confronts his *alter ego*. Dickens draws attention to the care with which he has laid the train of events by a fable, derived from *Tales of the Genii*, which occurs at the end of Chapter 38 immediately after Pip has at last seen Estella in her true colors and just before Magwitch returns to make a mockery of his expectations:

In the Eastern story, the heavy slab that was to fall on the bed of state in the flush of conquest was slowly wrought out of the quarry, the tunnel for the rope to hold it in its place was slowly carried through the leagues of rock, the slab was slowly raised and fitted in the roof, the rope was rove to it and slowly taken through the miles of hollow to the great iron ring. All being made ready with much labour, and the hour come, the sultan was roused in the dead of the night, and the sharpened axe that was to sever the rope from the great iron ring was put into his hand, and he struck with it, and the rope parted and rushed away, and the ceiling fell. So, in my case; all the work, near and afar, that tended to the end, had been accomplished; and in an instant the blow was struck, and the roof of my stronghold dropped upon me.

"You have made your own snares," Miss Havisham tells Pip on his last visit but one to Satis House. Ostensibly victimized by those who would use him for their own selfish ends, Pip is nevertheless led step by step, such is the compulsion of Dickens' narrative, to realize that every individual has a reciprocal share in the

wrongdoing of which he has been, however inno-
cently, the occasion. Estella is speaking for her lover
when she says in the revised ending that "suffering
has been stronger than all other teaching. . . ." And
it is for want of sufficient assurance, beyond her own
statement, that she has learned the same hard lesson,
that the original conclusion seems more commensu-
rate with the novel's design.

Despite Dickens' continuing dissatisfaction with
weekly serialization, its restrictions of scope imposed
on the later novels in this form an economy and coherence of organization which compensate for the
imaginative fertility of the more expansive works
which preceded them. *Hard Times*, *A Tale of Two
Cities*, and *Great Expectations* look forward to *The
Mystery of Edwin Drood*, which has some claim to be
considered the writer's most original narrative achievement, although its fragmentary state must forever
defy final critical assessment. On the other hand, *Little Dorrit* and *Our Mutual Friend*, the two final novels in twenty monthly parts, show unmistakable signs
that the writer's inventiveness had begun to flag under
the strain of devising and sustaining the great ramified
plot structures of earlier days. The involved exposi-
tion of Mrs. Clennam's secret not only taxes credulity,
but winds up the novel's central intrigue on an anti-
climactic note; and the overworking of the disguise
motif makes the Rokesmith-Bella plot of *Our Mutual
Friend* equally implausible. The technical aspects of
greatest interest in these novels relate to the grouping
of the extensive casts of characters and the prolifera-
tion of settings, as means of embodying the author's
darkening vision of his world. This is not to say, however, that the writer did not continue to tax his narrative resources for more effective means of projecting that vision.

Dickens experienced unusual difficulty in deciding on a story to support the critical purpose which was his point of departure in *Little Dorrit*. So much is apparent from Browne's cover, which depicts the primary thematic concerns of the novel, but does not, as in the design for *Dombey and Son*, suggest their investiture in concrete episodes. With the first part completed, the writer thought of starting over again in line with a new approach, which he described as follows to Forster: "It struck me that it would be a new thing to show people coming together, in a chance way, as fellow-travellers, and being in the same place, ignorant of one another, as happens in life; and to connect them afterwards, and to make the waiting for that connection a part of the interest." Since, however, the gathering in the quarantine station at Marseilles in Chapter 2 anticipates many of the future relationships beween characters, Dickens was unable to make full use of this idea, a Carlylean version of Goethe's doctrine of "elective affinities." The original title of the book, *Nobody's Fault*, retained through the first eleven chapters, suggests that at the outset political satire of the Circumlocution Office was paramount in the author's mind. Only with Amy Dorrit's entrance in the second number did the novel's scope broaden to include other targets of social criticism. And not until the sixth number did Dickens feel confident enough of the direction his story had taken to write to Forster: "Society, the Circumlocution Office, and Mr. Gowan, are, of course, three parts of one idea and design." In the chapter entitled "The History of a Self-Tormentor," Dickens reverted to the inserted tale. In justification of its insertion, he told Forster: "In Miss Wade I had an idea, which I thought a new one, of making the introduced story so fit into surroundings impossible of separation from the main story, as to make the blood of the book circulate through both." Since Miss Wade speaks for all the characters in the novel whose imprisonment within the confines of their egos is self-imposed, her disturbing confession is a brilliantly imaginative narrative device.

Our Mutual Friend, with its interweaving of the stories of two pairs of lovers of unequal station, is structurally the most ambitious of Dickens' novels. The twin narratives, polarized symbolically by the settings of the river and the dust-mounds, are so played off against each other as to arraign virtually every type of snobbish pretense ingrained in the Victorian class system. It is, however, in their conclusions that the last two novels on the grand scale most conclusively show that Dickens had learned to discipline his artistic conscience into conformity with the exigencies of plot. For here realism is no longer compromised by those conventional happy endings which in so many of the preceding stories provide for readers and characters alike an escape from the world as it has been represented. Joined in wedlock, Clennam and Amy Dorrit do not, like Woodcourt and Esther Summerson, withdraw to a retreat that has been prepared for them; but rather, as Dickens writes: "They went quietly down into the roaring streets, inseparable and blessed; and as they passed along in sunshine and shade, the noisy and the eager, and the arrogant and the froward and the vain, fretted, and chafed, and made their usual uproar." Rokesmith and Bella are permitted to enjoy the legacy accruing from the dust-mounds only after they have demonstrated that their happiness is not contingent on it; and Eugene, having abandoned the face-saving alternative of emigrating with Lizzie, proudly asserts: ". . . I will fight it out to the last gasp, with her and for her, here, in the open field."

FIVE

PRESENTATION OF CHARACTERS

If you want your public to believe in what you write you must believe in it yourself. When I am describing a scene I can as distinctly see what I am describing as I can see you now. So real are my characters to me that on one occasion I had fixed upon the course which one of them was to pursue. The character, however, got hold of me and made me do exactly the opposite to what I had intended; but I was so sure that he was right and I was wrong that I let him have his own way.

CHARLES DICKENS, QUOTED BY
HENRY FIELDING DICKENS
—*Harper's Monthly Magazine,*
CXXIX (1914)

It is remarkable that what we call the world, which is so very credulous in what professes to be true, is most incredulous in what professes to be imaginary; and that, while, every day in real life, it will allow in one man no blemishes, and in another no virtues, it will seldom admit a very strongly-marked character, either good or bad, in a fictitious narrative, to be within the limits of probability.

Nicholas Nickleby,
PREFACE

In seasons of pestilence, some of us will have a secret attraction to the disease— a terrible passing inclination to die of it. And all of us have like wonders hidden in our breasts, only needing circumstances to evoke them.

A Tale of Two Cities,
BOOK THREE,
CHAPTER 6

THE CHARACTERS IN DICKENS'
NOVELS ARE REAL IN THE
SAME WAY THAT CHARAC-
TERS IN PLAYS ARE REAL,
AND IN THE SAME WAY, PER-
HAPS, THAT LIVING PEOPLE
seem real to each other. Their true identities are
masked even from themselves under conventionally
prescribed poses, yet declare themselves through all
kinds of surface clues: not only in the overt act, but
in its accompanying gesture and facial expression; not
just in the spoken word, but in the intonation and
turn of speech with which it is uttered. Dickens'
method of characterization does not allow for the
delicate probing of psychological states of mind; rather
its success depends on the artist's resourcefulness in
creating consistent and emphatically defined patterns
of individualized responses to external circumstance;
in showing, that is to say, character in action.

Like Browning's Fra Lippo, whose "soul and sense"
grew "sharp alike" through early neglect, Dickens
might have traced to his waiflike boyhood in the
London streets his preternatural alertness to "the look
of things," the tokens of dress or mannerism which
differentiate one personage from another. But unless this acuity of vision had been tempered by the additional faculties of insatiable curiosity about human be-

havior and a genial, if sometimes caustic, sympathy with its oddities, the novelist would never have achieved the comprehensive humanity which informs his attitude towards his creatures. "His genius," Forster well remarked, "was his fellow feeling with his race; his mere personality was never the bound or limit to his perceptions, however strongly sometimes it might colour them. . . ."

Incredible though they often are, the beings who populate Dickens' stories command assent because of the vitality imparted to them by their creator's own transparent belief in their reality. "No man," according to Forster, "had ever so surprising a faculty as Dickens of becoming himself what he was representing . . ."; and the critic George Henry Lewes wrote: "Dickens once declared to me that every word said by his characters was distinctly *heard* by him. . . ." These statements are corroborated by Mary Dickens' account of seeing her father act out the fictional roles which he was imagining. The novelist's instructions to his illustrators are further evidence of the fact that his characters had assumed in the mind's eye the lineaments of living people. And frequent references to works in hand indicate the extent to which the writer became immersed in the lives of their characters. As he approached the end of *The Old Curiosity Shop*, he confessed to his future biographer: "I went to bed last night utterly dispirited and done up. All night I have been pursued by the child; and this morning I am unrefreshed and miserable." Of the emotional toll exacted by his Christmas book, "The Chimes," he wrote to Forster:

Since I conceived, at the beginning of the second part, what must happen in the third, I have undergone as much sorrow and agitation as if the thing were real; and have

wakened up with it at night. I was obliged to lock myself
in when I finished it yesterday, for my face was swollen
for the time to twice its proper size, and was hugely
ridiculous.

Forster is undoubtedly correct in associating Dickens'
closeness to his characters with his keen dramatic
sense:

He had the power of projecting himself into shapes and
suggestions of his fancy which is one of the marvels of
creative imagination, and what he desired to express he
became. The assumptions of the theatre have the same
method at a lower pitch, depending greatly on personal
accident; but the accident as much as the genius favoured
Dickens, and another man's conception underwent in his
acting the process which in writing he applied to his own.

E. M. Forster in *Aspects of the Novel* drew on
Dickens to illustrate his theoretical disapproval of
two-dimensional or "flat" characters. Yet, impressed
by the "wonderful feeling of human depth" conveyed
by many of these figures, he had to concede that the
novelist's "immense success with types suggests that
there may be more in flatness than the severer critics
admit." Forster's argument had in part been anticipated
by George Santayana in an important essay on
Dickens. No one has better described the conventional
point of view which finds it more comfortable to
pretend that Dickens is a mere caricaturist:

He was the perfect comedian. When people say Dickens
exaggerates, it seems to me they can have no eyes and
no ears. They probably have only *notions* of what things
and people are; they accept them conventionally, at their
diplomatic value. Their minds run on in the region of
discourse, where there are masks only and no faces, ideas
and no facts; they have little sense for those living
grimaces that play from moment to moment upon the

countenance of the world. The world is a perpetual caricature of itself; at every moment it is the mockery and the
contradiction of what it is pretending to be. But as it
nevertheless intends all the time to be something different
and highly dignified, at the next moment it corrects and
checks and tries to cover up the absurd thing it was; so
that a conventional world, a world of masks, is superimposed on the reality, and passes in every sphere of human
interest for the reality itself. Humour is the perception of
this illusion, the fact allowed to pierce here and there
through the convention, whilst the convention continues
to be maintained, as if we had not observed its absurdity.
Pure comedy is more radical, cruder, in a certain sense
less human; because comedy throws the convention over
altogether, revels for a moment in the fact, and brutally
says to the notions of mankind, as if it slapped them in
the face, There, take that! That's what you really are!
At this the polite world pretends to laugh, not tolerantly
as it does at humour, but a little angrily. It does not like
to see itself by chance in the glass, without having had
time to compose its features for demure self-contemplation. "What a bad mirror," it exclaims; "it must be concave or convex; for surely I never looked like that. Mere
caricature, farce and horse play. Dickens exaggerates; *I*
never was so sentimental as that; *I* never saw anything so
dreadful; *I* don't believe there were ever any people like
Quilp, or Squeers, or Serjeant Buzfuz." But the polite
world is lying; there *are* such people; we are such people
ourselves in our true moments, in our veritable impulses;
but we are careful to stifle and hide those moments from
ourselves and from the world; to purse and pucker ourselves into the mask of our conventional personality; and
so simpering, we profess that it is very coarse and inartistic of Dickens to undo our life's work for us in an instant and to remind us of what we are.

There is no reason to quarrel with Forster's assertion that Dickens' characters ultimately derive from
the "humours" of Jonsonian comedy;* but too much

* *Every Man in His Humour*, it will be remembered, was the
first play to be performed by Dickens' amateur company, with
the novelist himself in the part of Bobadill.

has been made of their typological aspect. Although Dickens did not work from living models, he often combined in one figure traits taken from different individuals, or, conversely, distributed among several characters the qualities observed in a single great eccentric. When the chiropodist, Mrs. Hill, protested against her portrait as Miss Mowcher in *David Copperfield,* Dickens retorted that all his characters "being made out of many people, were composite and never individual." Some of the foibles of John Dickens crop up in John Jarndyce and William Dorrit, as well as in Micawber. The originality which Dickens exercised in naming characters suggests that they were never conceived purely as types. Bumble and Bounderby and Pumblechook are all blustering and officious fools; but as the connotations of their names betoken, generic likeness is sunk in idiosyncratic aberrations from the norm.

Like seventeenth-century "humorous" characters and their progeny in the novels of Smollett and Fielding, the immortal comic and grotesque creations of Dickens' early period spring full-blown into existence, with no possibility or need for further growth. The scenes in which they appear are dramatically constructed to allow them to appear "in character," as it were. Thus it may be said that in the novels from *Pickwick Papers* to *Martin Chuzzlewit* the action reveals, but does not develop, character. Chesterton shrewdly observed of Dickens' practice at this time in his career: ". . . the *moving* machinery exists only to display entirely *static* character. Things in the Dickens story shift and change only in order to give us glimpses of great characters that do not change at all."

Chesterton's statement, however, does not make sufficient allowance for the surprise and pleasure attending progressive revelation. While characters certainly do not change in the sense that they are psychologically transformed, their experiences lead to behavior so unpredictable that growing familiarity is attended by a constant sense of discovery. This developing awareness, indeed, is a refraction of Dickens' own delight in creation. With regard to Pecksniff and Jonas Chuzzlewit he wrote Forster, while *Martin Chuzzlewit* was in progress:

As to the way in which these characters have opened out, that is to me one of the most surprising processes of the mind in this sort of invention. Given what one knows, what one does not know springs up; and I am as absolutely certain of its being true, as I am of the law of gravitation— if such a thing be possible—more so.

In Dickens' world character is never so inscrutable as the circumstances which bring out its inherent potentialities. Those two amiable buffoons, Dick Swiveller and Toots, need only to fall in love to become themselves lovable. And from that trio of limply fatuous aristocrats, Cousin Feenix, Sir Leicester Dedlock, and Twemlow, loyalty to the traditional values of their order calls forth a wholly admirable display of dignity.

Much as has been written about Dickens' supreme humorous figures, they resist critical analysis. Like their compeers, the great originals of Shakespearean comedy, they enjoy a free and autonomous life, uncircumscribed by the works in which they appear. Theirs is the license traditionally accorded the clown, whose antic disposition is a law unto itself. The Dickensian comic spirit is unfailingly embodied in histrionic guise. Its exemplars are self-declared fantasts, "of imagination all compact." They inhabit a world of their own making, a world which parodies, yet exists in total defiance of reality, a world in which the distinction between shadow and substance is turned topsy-turvy. At the outset stands Sam Weller with his inexhaustible store of analogues deriving from the absurd reactions of nonexistent beings caught in preposterous predicaments, and at the end there is Wegg, vicariously involved in the doings of his imaginary "Miss Elizabeth, Master George, Aunt Jane, and Uncle Parker." In between comes Sairey Gamp, not by any stretch of the fancy to be divorced from her fictitious confidante, Mrs. Harris.

These beings live by the power of the spoken word, though each has appropriated the resources of language for ends that subvert all habitual channels of communication. For them words are magic talismans, expressive of a perpetual state of wish-fulfillment, reordering actuality into conformity with felt needs. Dick Swiveller's idiom with its hodgepodge of music hall clichés provides the same escape from an impoverished present that Flora Finching finds in the lunatic disarray of her recollections. There is no disappointment for which Micawber cannot compensate by the triumphant exercise of his epistolary style.

Like Falstaff and the other clowns in Shakespeare, Dickens' comedians are fully self-aware. They enact their roles quite as much for their own delectation as to impose on their auditors, even though, as the novelist said, "My figures seem disposed to stagnate without crowds about them." "The great fool," Chesterton wrote, "is he in whom we cannot tell which is the conscious and which the unconscious humour." This ambiguity characterizes all of Dickens' greatest comic scenes, but none more than those in which Micawber appears. There is, for example, the unforgettable episode when David, about to part from his friends, re-

ceives the following lecture on the future conduct of
his affairs:

We had a very pleasant day, though we were all in a ten-
der state about our approaching separation.

"I shall never, Master Copperfield," said Mrs. Micawber, "revert to the period when Mr. Micawber was in
difficulties, without thinking of you. Your conduct has
always been of the most delicate and obliging description.
You have never been a lodger; you have been a friend."

"My dear," said Mr. Micawber, "Copperfield," for so
he had been accustomed to call me of late, "has a heart to
feel for the distresses of his fellow-creatures when they are
behind a cloud, and a head to plan, and a hand to—in
short, a general ability to dispose of such available property as could be made away with."

I expressed my sense of this commendation, and said
I was very sorry we were going to lose one another.

"My dear young friend," said Mr. Micawber, "I am
older than you; a man of some experience in life, and—
and of some experience, in short, in difficulties, generally
speaking. At present, and until something turns up (which
I am, I may say, hourly expecting), I have nothing to
bestow but advice. Still my advice is so far worth taking
that—in short, that I have never taken it myself, and am
the"—here Mr. Micawber, who had been beaming and
smiling, all over his head and face, up to the present moment, checked himself and frowned—"the miserable
wretch you behold."

"My dear Micawber!" urged his wife.

"I say," returned Mr. Micawber, quite forgetting himself and smiling again, "the miserable wretch you behold.
My advice is, never to do to-morrow what you can do
to-day. Procrastination is the thief of time. Collar him!"

"My poor papa's maxim," Mrs. Micawber observed.

"My dear," said Mr. Micawber, "your papa was very
well in his way, and Heaven forbid that I should dis-
parage him. Take him for all in all, we ne'er shall—in
short, make the acquaintance, probably, of anybody else
possessing, at his time of life, the same legs for gaiters,
and able to read the same description of print without
spectacles. But he applied that maxim to our marriage,

my dear; and that was so far prematurely entered into, in consequence, that I never recovered the expense."

Mr. Micawber looked aside at Mrs. Micawber, and added, "Not that I am sorry for it. Quite the contrary, my love." After that he was grave for a minute or so.

"My other piece of advice, Copperfield," said Mr. Micawber, "you know. Annual income twenty pounds, annual expenditure nineteen nineteen six, result happiness. Annual income twenty pounds, annual expenditure twenty pounds ought and six, result misery. The blossom is blighted, the leaf is withered, the God of day goes down upon the dreary scene, and—and in short you are for ever floored. As I am!"

To make his example more impressive, Mr. Micawber drank a glass of punch with an air of great enjoyment and satisfaction, and whistled the College Hornpipe.

The lesser comic characters in Dickens exhibit the same extraordinary resilience and imaginative supremacy over adversity, born of an unquenchable inclination to idealize reality. The novels are thronged with individuals who thus get along on theatrical make-believe. Their company includes such foolish widows as Mrs. Nickleby and Mrs. Sparsit; humble artisans whose fancies are related to their callings like Miss La Creevy and Jenny Wren; social impostors like Turveydrop and Mrs. General, with her fixation on the "formation of a surface"; would-be philosophers, such as the likable Captain Cuttle and the detestable Skimpole.

It is a recognized fact that Dickens' humorous vein runs most richly through the early novels. Its thinning out and turning acrid in the later work is commonly attributed to a decline in the exuberant optimism of the youthful years. But there are other reasons for this apparent loss of comic verve more closely allied with Dickens' artistic development. Professors Butt and Tillotson have shown in *Dickens at Work* that on the rare occasions in his later career when the novelist overwrote his monthly numbers, comic passages were always the first to be sacrificed to space requirements. The increasingly rigorous plot construction, first manifest in *Dombey and Son*, entailed a more functional view of characterization. Such characters as Major Bagstock, Bounderby, and Podsnap are creatures of their environments, giving lip service to the values on which worldly reputation depends. In contrast to the freedom enjoyed by their predecessors in the early stories who belong to no definable social class, these figures do not create for themselves private roles to satisfy the hunger of the imagination, but rather strut and fret through public parts, prescribed by their notion of what is expected of them. As a result, their playacting, expressive of the author's satiric intent, no longer provokes the untrammeled laughter of a Sam Weller or Mrs. Gamp or Micawber.

Strangely akin to these embodiments of the pure comic spirit are the grotesque villains of Dickens' early writings. Fagin, Squeers, Quilp, Pecksniff, even Uriah Heep, are only to be distinguished from their antic counterparts by a greater inclination and capacity to cause hurt. Like the clowns, their unfailing vivacity and resourcefulness constantly defy narrative restraint, so that the scenes in which they appear seem staged to release their sinister hilarity. Condemnable though these figures may be, moral reprobation sinks before the spectacle of Fagin schooling his gang of pickpockets, or Quilp bullying his wife by a display of indiscriminate voracity, or Pecksniff liquorishly fondling Mary Graham. For these characters also make an enduring appeal through their histrionic virtuosity. Old Martin Chuzzlewit is in reality paying grudging tribute to this faculty when he says to Pecksniff:

"Why, the annoying quality in *you*, is . . . that you never had a confederate or partner in *your* juggling; you would deceive everybody, even those who practise the same art; and have a way with you, as if you—he, he, he!—as if you really believed yourself. I'd lay a handsome wager now, . . . if I laid wagers, which I don't and never did, that you keep up appearances by a tacit understanding, even before your own daughters here. . . . You're not offended, Pecksniff?"

"Offended, my good sir!" cried that gentleman, as if he had received the highest compliments that language could convey.

In the later novels evil-doing, as has been said, is presented under an institutionalized aspect; and the villains, as a general rule, no longer exhibit the same malignant joy in wrong for its own sake. Already in *Barnaby Rudge*, Dennis the hangman condones his scoundrelism by appealing to the punitive legal system of which he is a minion; and so barefaced a malefactor as Blandois in *Little Dorrit* repeatedly insists that he is a gentleman who conducts himself no whit differently from respectable members of the business and professional classes. Yet, although the behavior of a Dombey or a Tulkinghorn or a Madame Defarge is in part explicable by class affiliation, the rampant evil in Dickens' world cannot finally be assimilated to any social system. There lurks at its heart an insoluble element suggestive of the novelist's ambivalent attitude toward the sources of human motivation.

Much of the time Dickens seems to have subscribed to the teaching of the political economists that individuals are shaped by environment. Monks' diabolical plot against Oliver is based on the assumption that the boy cannot avoid being contaminated by association with Fagin and his gang. "The wily old Jew," Dickens writes, "had the boy in his toils. Having prepared his

mind, by solitude and gloom, to prefer any society to
the companionship of his own sad thoughts in such
a dreary place, he was now slowly instilling into his
soul the poison which he hoped would blacken it, and
change its hue for ever." Similarly, of Nicholas
Nickleby's appalled recognition that Dotheboys Hall
is a spawning-ground for every kind of vice, the novelist says:

But the pupils—the young noblemen! How the last faint
traces of hope, the remotest glimmering of any good to
be derived from his efforts in this den, faded from the mind
of Nicholas as he looked in dismay around! Pale and
haggard faces, lank and bony figures, children with the
countenances of old men, deformities with irons upon
their limbs, boys of stunted growth, and others whose
long meagre legs would hardly bear their stooping bodies,
all crowded on the view together; there were the bleared
eye, the hare-lip, the crooked foot, and every ugliness of
distortion that told of unnatural aversion conceived by
parents for their offspring, or of young lives which, from
the earliest dawn of infancy, had been one horrible en-
durance of cruelty and neglect. There were little faces
which should have been handsome, darkened with the
scowl of sullen, dogged suffering; there was childhood
with the light of its eye quenched, its beauty gone, and
its helplessness alone remaining; there were vicious-faced
boys, brooding, with leaden eyes, like malefactors in a
jail; and there were young creatures on whom the sins
of their frail parents had descended, weeping even for
the mercenary nurses they had known, and lonesome
even in their loneliness. With every kindly sympathy
and affection blasted in its birth, with every young and
healthy feeling flogged and starved down, with every
revengeful passion that can foster in swollen hearts, eating
its evil way to their core in silence, what an incipient
Hell was breeding here!

The warped natures of Smike in *Nicholas Nickleby*
and of Hugh in *Barnaby Rudge* are alike referable to

early neglect and maltreatment. And in the Preface to *Martin Chuzzlewit* Dickens, somewhat unconvincingly, attempts to explain Jonas' criminal disposition on the same grounds:

I conceive that the sordid coarseness and brutality of Jonas would be unnatural, if there had been nothing in his early education, and in the precept and example always before him, to engender and develop the vices that make him odious. But, so born and so bred; admired for that which made him hateful, and justified from his cradle in cunning, treachery, and avarice; I claim him as the legitimate issue of the father upon whom those vices are seen to recoil.

At other times Dickens' division of his characters into camps, opposing unassailable virtue to immitigable depravity, points to an essentially Manichaean habit of mind. In answer to the charge that the portraiture of Sikes was too unrelieved in its darkness, the author offered the following tentative excuse in the Preface to *Oliver Twist:*

. . . I fear there are in the world some insensible and callous natures, that do become utterly and incurably bad. Whether this be so or not, of one thing I am certain: that there are such men as Sikes, who, being closely followed through the same space of time and through the same current of circumstances, would not give, by the action of a moment, the faintest indication of a better nature.

In the same novel the half brothers, Monks and Oliver, stand in implausibly stark contrast. The malevolent motivation of the one is as incomprehensible as is the other's innate innocence, given the conditions under which he grows up. A similar polarity of moral absolutes creates an unbridgeable gulf between Quilp and Nell in *The Old Curiosity Shop.*

Sceptical of organized charity and all other official agencies for reform, Dickens relied on individual benevolence to relieve suffering and misfortune. In the early novels, as has been noted, this mission is entrusted to the company of affluent and compassionate elders which includes Pickwick, Brownlow, the Cheeryble brothers, Garland, old Martin Chuzzlewit, Betsey Trotwood, and John Jarndyce. Although the Cheeryble brothers were inspired by a pair of philanthropic Manchester industrialists, Dickens' portrayal of this type is so deliberately lacking in realism that one may doubt whether its exemplars were ever actual to their creator in other than a symbolic sense. Their Olympian hovering over the action of the stories, on which they fortuitously intervene at opportune moments, suggests that they belong to a transcendent order representative of ideal charity. Esther Summerson, indeed, acknowledges as much when she admits at the end of *Bleak House* to feeling towards John Jarndyce "as if he were a superior being. . . ."

Dickens' growing insight during the 1840s into the organic constitution of Victorian society led to important developments in his methods of presenting character, as well as to the perfecting of his narrative art. A shift in perspective is reflected in the very titles of the later novels. In contrast to the early works named after their protagonists, *Bleak House*, *Hard Times*, *A Tale of Two Cities*, *Nobody's Fault* (the original title of *Little Dorrit*), *Great Expectations*, and *Our Mutual Friend* call attention to the new emphasis on theme within an expanding social focus. Edmund Wilson was the first to point out that Dickens originated "a new literary genre . . . the novel of the social group." Beginning with *Dombey and Son*, there is an increasing interaction between characters and their cultural milieu. Motivation is determined more by environmental pressures and less by the impulses of the isolated and unrestrained ego. Society has assumed the role of corporate villain, and individual malefactions are made to seem symptomatic of prevalent abuses. The victimized child is a recurrent figure in Dickens' fiction from his earliest work; but in the mature novels the all but universal neglect or abuse of children by their parents is systematically elaborated as one of the signs of the times. Dombey's pride, so fatal to the happiness of his family, is a *class* pride, typifying the irresponsible exercise of authority by those in positions of rank and power. The novelist ironically poses the question: "Was Mr. Dombey's master-vice, that ruled him so inexorably, an unnatural characteristic?" And he goes on: "It might be worth while, sometimes, to inquire what Nature is, and how men work to change her, and whether, in the enforced distortions so produced, it is not natural to be unnatural." Given a social order dedicated to the perversion of all natural bonds, there is little to choose between Dombey and all the other heartlessly self-infatuated parents, including Mrs. Jellyby, Gradgrind, William Dorrit, Podsnap.

Such is the power of institutionalized evil in these later novels that individual philanthropy is of little avail. John Jarndyce is helpless to safeguard his wards, and Boffin seems almost to have been conceived as a parody of the Pickwickian savior. In Dickens' early work, charity exists as a transcendent ideal, invading the stories from outside in the persons of altruistic, but essentially disengaged, benefactors. Florence Dombey signalizes the emergence of a new type to embody the regenerative power of love, now represented as inhering within the social scene. She is the first of the suffering girl heroines who play a redemptive role in most of the subsequent novels. The category includes, in addition to Florence, Agnes Wickfield, Esther Summerson, Sissy Jupe, Amy Dorrit, Lizzie Hexam.

There is an unmistakable family likeness among these characters. A development from the lost children, Oliver Twist and Nell, of the earlier works, they exhibit in fusion a number of traditional strains associated with the archetypal figure of the saintly innocent, as variously endorsed by New Testament Christianity and the romantic glorification of childhood.* In virtually every respect, save incorruptibility of heart, they stand at the farthest remove from the images of paternal benignity. Whereas Pickwick and his successors are aging and securely prosperous members of the middle class, these figures are young girls, usually destitute and invariably unprotected. Esther is illegitimate; Sissy and Lizzie come from the dregs of society and are illiterate. All have lost their mothers and have been neglected or otherwise mistreated by fathers or surrogate parents. They resemble each other in additional ways, which doubtless reflect Dickens' dislike of his own disorderly family life. They share with their creator, for example, a kind of passion for tidiness in their domestic arrangements. Of Nell, who is in many ways the progenitor of the type, Gissing wrote: "From the beginning of the story, when she is seen making order and comfort in the gloomy old house, to the end of her wanderings in the cottage by

---

* The type can be enlarged to include the actual fools who so often originate or are the occasion for meritorious actions in Dickens' fiction: Smike, Barnaby Rudge, Mr. Dick, Maggy in *Little Dorrit*, perhaps even Joe Gargery. Henry James, who was less than sympathetic with these characters, wrote of Jenny Wren in his review of *Our Mutual Friend:* "Like all Mr. Dickens's pathetic characters, she is a little monster; . . . she belongs to the troop of hunchbacks, imbeciles, and precocious children, who have carried on the sentimental business in all Mr. Dickens's novels; the little Nells, the Smikes, the Paul Dombeys."

the still churchyard, her one desire is for the peace and security of home." Furthermore, like Nell, Dickens' later heroines habitually reverse the customary pattern of familial responsibility, the daughter assuming the place of mother and wife to the erring father. In every case the sovereign virtue which enables these beings to remain irreproachably immaculate amidst all the evil which environs them is a spiritual holiness based on unreflecting trust in divine providence. And their indubitable role in their respective narratives is to embody the dynamic power of love, as a touchstone for making moral discriminations among the actions of all the other characters.

Although Dickens' girl heroines are much more vitally involved in their stories than the patriarchal benefactors whom they replace, they, like all of the novelist's creatures who conform to type, are conceived in fundamentally static terms. They are, however, frequently played off against a very different kind of female character who testifies to Dickens' growing concern with the psychological grounds of internal conflict. For the later novels present a remarkable series of women of passionate temperament, whose outbursts of feeling and reckless actions signify divided natures. They all, for one reason or another, have been humiliated, placed on the defensive, and relegated to the position of outsiders by society, with which they seek to get even for their wounded self-esteem. Their number includes Edith Dombey, Rosa Dartle, Lady Dedlock and Hortense, Louisa Gradgrind, Fanny Dorrit, Miss Wade and Tattycoram, and, with significant differences, Estella and Bella Wilfer. Whether innocent or guilty, all these fear, while at the same time they resent and defy, the tyranny of opinion. The sympathy which they in part compel as victims under a moral code inequitable in its oppression of their sex is counteracted by their erratic response to fancied grievances. For all, like Miss Wade, are neurotic self-tormentors, riven between hatred against those who have used them and against themselves for submitting to be so used. Dickens, however, could never rival Richardson or Charlotte Brontë in fineness of insight into the feminine nature; and the interest which these characters arouse is dissipated through such anti-climactic scenes as that between Edith Dombey and Carker, or Rosa Dartle and Em'ly, or Louisa Grad-grind and her father on the night of Harthouse's attempted seduction.

Forster perceptively observed of Dickens' methods of characterization that

no man could better adjust the outward and visible oddi-ties in a delineation to its inner and unchangeable veraci-ties. The rough estimates we form of character, if we have any truth of perception, are on the whole correct: but men touch and interfere with one another by the contact of their extremes, and it may very often become necessarily the main business of a novelist to display the salient points, the sharp angles, or the prominences merely.

While generally true enough, this statement fails to take into account Dickens' fascination with the phe-nomenon of split personality or to give credit to his techniques for dramatizing the buried motives which individuals keep hidden from the world and even from themselves. That the writer had developed to a high degree the faculty of self-disassociation and was cap-able of dispassionately probing his own subliminal states of mind is apparent from his occasional writ-ings. In "A Fly-Leaf in a Life" from *The Uncommer-cial Traveller* he speaks of "Being accustomed to ob-serve myself as curiously as if I were another man . . ."; and a second piece, entitled "Lying Awake," gives an astonishing display of the power of autosuggestion on the passive mentality. Not surprisingly, then, in his more searching character studies, Dickens takes account of the conditions of imaginative awareness which lie on the borderline between the conscious and the unconscious and which find expression in dreams and related states.

Dickens' use of dreams for fictional purposes is extremely sophisticated, anticipating in many respects the findings of Freud. He is especially original in exploiting what may be called the waking dream, in which impressions derived from the surrounding world merge with subjective imaginings. Oliver Twist undergoes two such experiences, which leave in their wake an intuitive sense of the evil threatening him. The first occurs in Chapter 9 when Oliver "in a drowsy state, between sleeping and waking" beholds Fagin sorting over the jewelry which includes the trinket once in the possession of the boy's dead mother. "At such times," the author comments, "a mortal knows just enough of what his mind is doing, to form some glimmering conception of its mighty powers, its bounding from earth and spurning time and space, when freed from the restraint of its corporeal associate." The second and more sinister episode comes in Chapter 34. Oliver's new-found security in the Maylie household is shattered when he awakens from a nap to the certainty that Fagin and Monks have been watching him through the open window. The scene is prefaced by this passage:

There is a kind of sleep that steals upon us sometimes, which while it holds the body prisoner, does not free the mind from a sense of things about it, and enable it to ramble at its pleasure. So far as an overpowering heaviness, a prostration of strength, and an utter inability to control our thoughts or power of motion, can be called sleep, this is it; and yet, we have a consciousness of all that is going on about us, and, if we dream at such a time, words which are really spoken, or sounds which really exist at the moment, accommodate themselves with surprising readiness to our visions, until reality and imagination become so strangely blended that it is afterwards almost a matter of impossibility to separate the two. Nor is this, the most striking phenomenon incidental to such a state. It is an undoubted fact, that although our sense of touch and sight be for the time dead, yet our sleeping thoughts, and the visionary scenes that pass before us, will be influenced and materially influenced, by the *mere silent presence* of some external object; which may not have been near us when we closed our eyes: and of whose vicinity we have had no waking consciousness.

Equally ambiguous in their implications are the distorted images of actuality that penetrate the drowsing minds of Nell, frightened by the nocturnal apparition of her father in the grip of his mania, and of Stephen Blackpool holding vigil over his drunken wife.

Allied with the dream state are the hallucinations which may torment the imagination under extreme emotional stress. Pip prophetically foresees Miss Havisham's death in the hanging effigy that appears to him on his first visit to Satis House. And memories of their long years of imprisonment come back to unsettle the minds of William Dorrit in his final collapse at Rome and Dr. Manette after Lucy's marriage. Differing in effect but equally revelatory of conflicting levels of apprehension are the watery visions which precede Paul Dombey's death and which shadow Eugene Wrayburn's struggle to survive. Betty Higden

Another device for dramatically projecting the warring impulses in man's nature, and one which particularly appealed to Dickens' imagination, is that of doubling. Sometimes, as in the case of Flintwinch and his twin brother, the novelist uses similarity in ap-

pearance merely as a narrative contrivance. More often,
however, a character recognizes in his double the
more ideal or the more degraded half of his divided
being. Thus, Sydney Carton confronts his better
nature in Charles Darnay; and Edith Dombey's discovery of spiritual kinship with the fallen Alice Mar-
wood provokes the surmise: "In this round world of
many circles within circles, do we make a weary journey from the high grade to the low, to find at last
that they lie close together, that the two extremes
touch, and that our journey's end is but our starting-
place?"

These graphic methods of bringing to the surface
that clandestine other self which lurks in the inner
recesses of being are displayed with special adroitness
in the depictions of criminal behavior which are by
general agreement Dickens' psychological master-
pieces. R. H. Hutton, one of the novelist's earliest and
most sagacious critics, declared: "No author indeed
could draw more powerfully than he the mood of a
man haunted by a fixed idea, a shadowy apprehension,
a fear, a dream, a remorse. . . ." And calling attention
to Dickens' success in presenting "the restlessness of a
murderer," Hutton comments on his knowledge of
"the sort of supremacy which a given idea gets over the
mind in a dream, and in those waking states of nervous
apprehension akin to dreams." Dream psychology is
strikingly used to differentiate between two contrasting kinds of criminal mentality in the nightmares which
visit Montague Tigg and Jonas Chuzzlewit on the eve
of the murder of one by the other. Jonas, furthermore,
is paralyzed by the hallucinatory conviction that he
has become two separate individuals, as he prepares,
after his deed of violence, to return to the room from
which he set out in disguise:

Dread and fear were upon him. To an extent he had never counted on, and could not manage in the least degree. He was so horribly afraid of that infernal room at home. This made him, in a gloomy, murderous, mad way, not only fearful *for* himself but *of* himself; for being, as it were, a part of the room: a something supposed to be there, yet missing from it: he invested himself with its mysterious terrors; and when he pictured in his mind the ugly chamber, false and quiet, false and quiet, through the dark hours of two nights; and the tumbled bed, and he not in it, though believed to be; he became in a manner his own ghost and phantom, and was at once the haunting spirit and the haunted man.

In like manner, subjective and objective reality intermingle and are confused in the visions that accompany the headlong flights of Sikes and Carker; and the staring eyes of the dog that drive Sikes over the parapet and the rushing of the engine that dismembers Carker gradually take on for the reader the same unearthly significance lent them in the demented imaginations of the transgressors.

Lady Dedlock, Bradley Headstone, and John Jasper brilliantly exemplify Dickens' handling of the device of doubling to project complexity of motivation in narrative terms. The true nature of each is revealed through the disguises that he assumes. At different times Lady Dedlock is identified with her fierce maidservant Hortense and Jenny, the brickmaker's wife. The first deception helps create suspense about the perpetrator of Tulkinghorn's murder; the second serves to prolong the chase which fatally terminates at the gates of the burial ground. At a deeper metaphorical level, however, the two characters for whom Lady Dedlock is mistaken represent the felonious and conscience-stricken impulses contending in her breast. Hortense in a very real sense is her symbolic agent in settling accounts with the lawyer who has discovered her secret. In changing garb with Jenny, Lady Dedlock not only tacitly acquiesces to the common tie which unites all forlorn mothers, but symbolically atones for her failure in love toward her own daughter.

Bradley Headstone's plot to pin suspicion on Rogue Riderhood is a subtle elaboration of Hortense's similar scheme with regard to Lady Dedlock. Of Bradley clad in his schoolmaster's attire the author writes that "there was a certain stiffness in his manner of wearing this, as if there were a want of adaptation between him and it. . . ." When he masquerades as Riderhood, however, Dickens says: "And whereas, in his own schoolmaster's clothes, he usually looked as if they were the clothes of some other man, he now looked in the clothes of some other man, or men, as if they were his own." Bradley's hope that he can return to his old self by shedding the incriminating raiment is as unavailing as are his efforts to put behind him the crime which he perpetually reenacts in his thoughts. Riderhood's arrival to taunt him with the evidence of his duplicity precipitates the teacher's symbolic gesture of erasing his name which he has written on the blackboard. The denouement follows with inflexible logic; for the circumstances of their deaths seal the fellowship of these twin spirits.

The Mystery of Edwin Drood, even in its unfinished form, carries to still more refined extremes Dickens' exploration of the mysterious incongruities in human motivation. The characterization of John Jasper, lay precentor of Cloisterham Cathedral and opium-eater, melodious singer and strangler, anticipates Stevenson's *Dr. Jekyll and Mr. Hyde*. For in this schizophrenic the two selves are fully internalized, and the conflict between good and evil is traced to its ultimate source in the irreconcilable duality of human nature.

No one has presented the corrosive effects of guilt more vividly than Dickens. It, more than any other force, motivates change, whether for better or worse, in those of his characters who are not merely static. Dickens' villains are customarily destroyed by guilt, just as his protagonists are redeemed by its operation. It works, however, in different ways, being an effect of wicked actions, but a cause of noble conduct. Its destructive power is manifest in Dickens' earliest delineations of criminals, a Sikes or Ralph Nickleby. Not until relatively late in his career did he succeed, largely through its instrumentality, in creating psychologically convincing roles for the heroes of his stories.

The youthful "leads" who give their names to the early novels or who are nominally apportioned prominent parts in them, Nicholas Nickleby, Kit Nubbles, Jo Willett, Martin Chuzzlewit, Walter Gay, remain for the most part insubstantial figures. Bourgeois variations on the *picaro* seeking his fortune through adversity, they emerge unscathed from their adventures to enjoy the reward of the conventional happy ending. David Copperfield is the first of Dickens' protagonists who recognizably grows to maturity as a result of the trials he passes through. His characterization is the combined result of Dickens' deepened social awareness and of his need to impose a meaningful pattern on his own early experiences. In this novel, furthermore, Dickens first seriously confronted a challenge which he shared with other Victorian novelists: namely, the problem of locating within the context of contemporary manners and morals the grounds for heroic action. His solution to this problem, paralleling similar efforts by Thackeray, Trollope, and Meredith, was to seek to redefine the traditional concept of the gentleman in conformity with Victorian ideals. In David's eyes, it is Steerforth and not himself who is the hero of the story through half its course. And, indeed, the two figures strangely complement each other. Both exhibit a certain ruthlessness in pursuing their ends. Without the narrator's proneness to self-delusion, Steerforth lacks the saving grace of fellow-feeling for the sensibilities of others which mitigates David's weakness. His egoism and readiness to capitalize on his personal charm and the prerogatives of social rank reappear in such gentlemen *manqués* as Harthouse in *Hard Times* and Henry Gowan in *Little Dorrit*. On the other hand, Steerforth repays David's idolatry with genuine, if condescending, affection; and he is sufficiently shamefaced over his failure to live up to the image he has instilled in David's heart to part with him before the final betrayal. If Steerforth so often usurps interest from the protagonist, it is because his conduct exhibits signs of inner stresses of conscience from which David is exempt as a result of the better fortune contrived for him.

Richard Carstone, whose deterioration under the seductive vision of unmerited gain carried out the author's original plan for Walter Gay, is a transitional figure, anticipating the more complexly motivated protagonists of subsequent novels. Arthur Clennam, Sydney Carton, Pip, and Eugene Wrayburn are inheritors of Richard's well-meaning, but vacillating, nature. Like him, also, they nurture undefined, although deeply ingrained, feelings of guilt, which relate them in many ways to the malefactors for whom Dickens compels sympathy. It was one of the novelist's great original insights that unjust treatment may be fully as effective as actual wrongdoing in arousing feelings of remorse and self-doubt. In *The Old Curiosity Shop* Kit Nubbles' anguish at being falsely accused occasions the following passage of commentary:

Let moralists and philosophers say what they may, it is very questionable whether a guilty man would have felt half as much misery that night, as Kit did, being innocent. The world, being in the constant commission of vast quantities of injustice, is a little too apt to comfort itself with the idea that if the victim of its falsehood and malice have a clear conscience, he cannot fail to be sustained under his trials, and somehow or other to come right at last; "in which case," say they who have hunted him down, "—though we certainly don't expect it—nobody will be better pleased than we." Whereas, the world would do well to reflect, that injustice is in itself, to every generous and properly constituted mind, an injury, of all others the most insufferable, the most torturing, and the most hard to bear; and that many clear consciences have gone to their account elsewhere, and many sound hearts have broken, because of this very reason; the knowledge of their own deserts only aggravating their sufferings, and rendering them the less endurable.

Although reproachless, Florence Dombey cannot shed the conviction that she is somehow to blame for her father's hostility. Of the state of mind which ensued on his brutal whipping by Murdstone, David Copperfield says: "My stripes were sore and stiff, and made me cry afresh, when I moved; but they were nothing to the guilt I felt. It lay heavier on my breast than if I had been a most atrocious criminal, I dare say." And Pip nurses a residue of self-recrimination as a result of his sister's harsh treatment.

Guilt, instilled by injustice, has in Dickens' view the invariable effect of paralyzing the wills of its victims. The resulting apathy, made up in equal measure of self-pity and distrust of active engagement in outside affairs, is brilliantly exemplified by the narrator of the strange short story entitled, "George Silverman's Explanation," as well as in Miss Wade's "The History of a Self-Tormentor." Such poseurs as Harthouse and Gowan and Bentley Drummle make much of this lassitude as an aspect of their gentlemanly pretensions. The self-lacerating habit of mind which it induces in more consequential figures is most penetratingly explored in *Little Dorrit*, where it is associated not only with Mrs. Clennam's gloomy Calvinism, but with all the other socially sanctioned forms of egoism which incapacitate the characters in this novel. William Dorrit is not less disabled by his assumption of grandeur than Merdle is by his false eminence as a financier or Casby by his patriarchal posture or Miss Wade by her masochistic delusions.

Humphry House noted that Dickens' view of human nature does not allow for the concept of original sin. Its place is taken by the complex of penitential feelings which enmesh the novelist's most deeply studied characters—feelings which, although they originate in some private conviction of failure or insufficiency, carry with them a sense of responsibility for the evil perpetrated by others. As a result, for all these individuals the inertia imposed by the self-inflicted consciousness of guilt seeks release in acts of vicarious atonement for the actual guilt of others. Arthur takes on himself the burden of Mrs. Clennam's unrevealed secret, and Rokesmith sacrifices his inheritance to make amends for the eccentric provisions of old Harmon's will.

In Dickens' world love is the only force strong enough to burst the bonds of the imprisoning ego and to release the capacity for genuinely altruistic action. This is not the divisive sexual passion which is really another form of self-love. A late discovery in Dickens' fiction, its power destroys Bradley Headstone and John Jasper, leading to deeds of violence which only confirm their dreadful isolation from their kind. The characters who achieve self-transcendence are the ones who undergo a change of heart, having learned through suffering to prefer a good other than their own.

Allegorical implications hover over Dickens' representations of spiritual redemption. Although most clearly announced in *A Tale of Two Cities*,* the theme of resurrection is common to all the late novels. *Dombey and Son* first establishes a recurrent pattern in which the regeneration of a central character is preceded by a period of illness or nervous disorder. Florence Dombey saves her father from suicide. David Copperfield is free to seek out Agnes only after a period of probation in Switzerland. Arthur Clennam undergoes purgation in the Marshalsea. Joe Gargery returns to nurse Pip through the sickness which ensues on Magwitch's death. John Rokesmith emerges with a new identity from near-drowning; and Eugene Wrayburn, broken in body and spirit, is quite literally reborn. In each instance, recovery conforms to the stages in the experience of conversion. The individual, having passed through his dark night of despair, affirms his recovery by some deed of expiation. These deeds are manifold in their points of moral reference; they may be motivated by a desire on the doer's part

---

* The fact cannot be too strongly emphasized, however, that Dickens invariably took pains to knit his thematic concerns into the texture of the narrative proper. For example, the expectations raised by Jarvis Lorry's password, "Recalled to Life" at the start of *A Tale of Two Cities*, are circumstantially satisfied by the recovery of Dr. Manette. It is only in the context of the entire train of events leading up to Sydney Carton's heroic sacrifice that the phrase takes on full metaphorical significance. The same is true for the splendid irony of the remark made at the end of Chapter 2 by Jerry Cruncher, whose gruesome calling as a Resurrection-Man has yet to be revealed: " 'Recalled to life.' That's a Blazing strange message. Much of that wouldn't do for you, Jerry! I say, Jerry! You'd be in a Blazing bad way, if recalling to life was to come into fashion, Jerry!"

to compensate for his own past transgressions; but in their salvific effects on the lives of others they incarnate the triumph of love over evil. Thus, Sydney Carton's death, in saving the husband of his beloved, at the same time redeems both the inhumanity of Darnay's aristocratic forbears and, more directly through his kindness to the seamstress, the matching inhumanity of the revolutionary tribunal. By succoring Magwitch, Pip does not simply repay in full his debt to his benefactor, but makes up for Compeyson's betrayal of Magwitch and his own of Joe.

The cases of Clennam and Wrayburn are slightly different, since each is tangibly recompensed for his transformation (as is also true for Pip in the revised ending of *Great Expectations*). Yet, each acts without expecting reward; and neither story, as has been pointed out, can be said to end in unclouded felicity. For in rededicating themselves to the happiness of Amy Dorrit and Lizzie Hexam, both Arthur and Eugene bring to their unions the contrite knowledge that through their own previous misprisal of the treasures of devotion offered them, they have helped confirm the martyr's role reserved for saints in this world. Nevertheless, Dickens is finally saying that salvation from the blight of the social will can only come through the reconstitution of the individual will by love.

SIX
USE OF SETTING

*We are so much in the habit of allowing impressions to
be made upon us by external objects, which should be produced by reflection alone, but which, without such
visible aids, often escape us, that I am not sure I should
have been so thoroughly
possessed by this one*   The Old Curiosity Shop,
subject, but for the heaps   CHAPTER I
*of fantastic things I had
seen huddled together in the curiosity-dealer's warehouse.
These, crowding on my mind, in connection with the
child, and gathering round her, as it were, brought
her condition palpably before me.*

*In Bleak House, I have purposely dwelt upon the
romantic side of familiar
things.*   Bleak House, PREFACE

*The whole idea of the story is sufficiently difficult to
require the most exact truth and the greatest knowledge
and skill in the colouring throughout. . . . the little
subtle touches of description which, by making the
country house and the general scene real, would give an
air of reality to the people
(much to be desired), are*   LETTER FROM CHARLES DICKENS
altogether wanting. The   TO EMILY JOLLY
more you set yourself to the   — MAY 30, 1857
*illustration of your heroine's
passionate nature, the more indispensable this attendant
atmosphere of truth becomes. It would . . . oblige the
reader to believe in her. Whereas, for ever exploding like
a great firework without any background, she glares and
wheels and hisses, and goes out, and has lighted nothing.*

ETTING IS AN INSEPAR-
ABLE COMPONENT BOTH OF
DICKENS' NARRATIVE ART-
ISTRY AND OF HIS METHODS
OF CHARACTERIZATION. IN-
DEED, THE MOST LASTINGLY
memorable quality of the novels may well be their
atmospheric density, wrought from the stylistic bril-
liance of the descriptive writing. Chesterton believed
it "characteristic of Dickens that his atmospheres are
more important than his stories." Speaking of the
"atmosphere of mystery and wrong . . . which
gathers round Mrs. Clennam, rigid in her chair, or old
Miss Havisham, ironically robed as a bride," the same
critic concludes that it "altogether eclipses the story
which often seems disappointing in comparison." The
mere enumeration of the great dramatic scenes in
Dickens conjures up the places where they occur with
all the attendant circumstances. Many actions which
would otherwise seem outrageously melodramatic
command a "willing suspension of disbelief," so sharp
is the author's eye for the relevant detail and so tangible
is its rendering. The point may be exemplified by any
of the passages showing characters in headlong flight
—one of Dickens' favorite methods of bringing his
stories to a climax. Examples are Sikes' wanderings

after the murder of Nancy, Nell's evasion of Quilp,
Carker's departure from Dijon, David's escape from
London to Dover, Lady Dedlock's disappearance, Pip's
journey down the Thames with Magwitch. Slight but
telltale descriptive touches impart conviction to each
of these episodes: as when Sikes finds momentary
respite from guilt in fighting the fire, or Nell is suc-
cored by the stoker, or the beggars solicit Carker, or
David lurks timorously outside the den of the ogre-
like clothing dealer, or Bucket furtively consults the
Thames police, or Pip is alerted to Compeyson's pursuit by the "Jack" of the causeway. With regard to
this passage in *Great Expectations* Forster relates an
informative anecdote, indicative of the novelist's
scrupulous attention to factual accuracy:

At the opening of the story there had been an exciting
scene of the wretched man's chase and recapture among
the marshes, and this has its parallel at the close in his
chase and recapture on the river while poor Pip is helping
to get him off. To make himself sure of the actual course
of a boat in such circumstances, and what possible incidents the adventure might have, Dickens hired a steamer
for the day from Blackwall to Southend. Eight or nine
friends and three or four members of his family were on
board, and he seemed to have no care, the whole of that
summer day (22nd of May, 1861), except to enjoy their
enjoyment and entertain them with his own in shape of a
thousand whims and fancies; but his sleepless observation
was at work all the time, and nothing had escaped his
keen vision on either side of the river.

Dickens habitually relies on setting to convey
truths which the conventions of the time debarred him
from expressing more openly by means of narrative
and dialogue. Gissing observed that "London as a
place of squalid mystery and terror, of the grimly
grotesque, of labyrinthine obscurity and lurid fascina-

tion is Dickens's own. . . ." With *Oliver Twist* the writer set out, in declared opposition to the romanticizing proclivities of Harrison Ainsworth and others of the so-called "Newgate" writers, to portray the criminal underworld of St. Giles and Saffron Hill in all its unspeakable degradation. The 1841 Preface explicitly sets forth his intent:

I had read of thieves by scores—seductive fellows (amiable for the most part), faultless in dress, plump in pocket, choice in horseflesh, bold in bearing, fortunate in gallantry, great at a song, a bottle, pack of cards or dice-box, and fit companions for the bravest. But I had never met (except in HOGARTH) with the miserable reality. It appeared to me that to draw a knot of such associates in crime as really do exist; to paint them in all their deformity, in all their wretchedness, in all the squalid poverty of their lives; to shew them as they really are, for ever skulking uneasily through the dirtiest paths of life, with the great, black, ghastly gallows closing up their prospect, turn them where they may; it appeared to me that to do this, would be to attempt a something which was greatly needed, and which would be a service to society. And therefore I did it as I best could . . .

What manner of life is that which is described in these pages, as the every-day existence of a Thief? What charms has it for the young and ill-disposed, what allurements for the most jolter-headed of juveniles? Here are no canterings on moonlit heaths, no merry-makings in the snuggest of all possible caverns, none of the attractions of dress, no embroidery, no lace, no jack-boots, no crimson coats and ruffles, none of the dash and freedom with which 'the road' has been, time out of mind, invested. The cold, wet, shelterless midnight streets of London; the foul and frowsy dens, where vice is closely packed and lacks the room to turn; the haunts of hunger and disease; the shabby rags that scarcely hold together: where are the attractions of these things?

If, without offending the sensibilities of Victorian readers by the language and doings of his thieves and whores, Dickens was yet so largely successful in his determination not to "abate one hole in the Dodger's coat or one scrap of curl-paper in Nancy's dishevelled hair," this achievement must be laid to the suggestive power of the setting. Dickens knew that if the background of his story was sketched in convincingly enough, the rest might be left to inference. Again it is Gissing who perceives what the novelist is about: "The point to be kept in view regarding these ideal characters is that, however little their speech and conduct may smack of earth, their worldly surroundings are shown with marvelous fidelity."

Often it is impossible to impute any existence to Dickens' characters outside the milieus which they seem to have spun about themselves like cocoons. This holds especially for the great eccentrics; so that, for example, Mrs. Jarley is unimaginable apart from her caravan, or Captain Cuttle from the Wooden Midshipman, or Venus from his gallery of stuffed horrors. With major figures, however, environment becomes a means not only for emphasizing individuality, but also for determining motive and act. Dickens rivals Balzac in his capacity to describe dwellings every facet of which is revelatory of the inhabitants' lives. Wonderfully discriminated are Chesney Wold, Mrs. Clennam's home, and Satis House, all decaying and each the habitat of a doomed woman immured with her dark secret. The residences of Dombey, Gradgrind, Merdle, Podsnap, and the Veneerings through their physical properties alone arraign the qualities that Dickens reprehended in their owners. All disclose the same attachment to material well-being, evidenced by the tastelessly over-furnished rooms, the lavishly indigestible meals, the pompous routine of joyless entertainments. Yet each has its own personality, mirroring the variation from type of its inmate. There is no confusing Merdle's Chief Butler with the Analytical Chemist who presides over Veneering's table, so sensitively is the brand of servile snobbery flaunted by each in tune with the social pretentions of the establishment in which he is employed. At a deeper level of apprehension, Florence Dombey, Louisa Gradgrind, Amy Dorrit (in Venice and Rome), and Georgiana Podsnap suffer intolerable loneliness in homes which seem to them actual physical extensions of the different shades of neglect inflicted by their fathers.*

A distinguishing characteristic of Dickens' descriptions is their fanciful mingling of the animate and inanimate, as if to imply that a reciprocal relationship exists between beings and their surroundings. This

---

* Because of the close collaboration between writer and artist, the illustrations of the works repay close study as indices of Dickens' dependence on the visual response of readers to his settings. His constant instructions to the various illustrators attest the novelist's concern that the graphic representations of scenes absolutely conform to his conceptions. In criticism of the initial sketch depicting the parlor in which Mrs. Corney entertains Bumble, he wrote to Cruikshank: "I have described a *small* kettle for one on the fire—a *small* black teapot on the table with a little tray & so forth—and a two ounce tin tea cannister. Also a shawl hanging up—and the cat and kittens before the fire." And to Forster he forcibly voiced his dissatisfaction with Hablot Browne's treatment of a scene from *Dombey and Son:* "I am really *distressed* by the illustration of Mrs. Pipchin and Paul. It is so frightfully and wildly wide of the mark. Good Heaven! in the commonest and most literal construction of the text, it is all wrong. She is described as an old lady, and Paul's 'miniature armchair' is mentioned more than once. He ought to be sitting in a little arm-chair down in the corner of the fireplace, staring up at her. I can't say what pain and vexation it is to be so utterly misrepresented. I would cheerfully have given a hundred pounds to have kept this illustration out of the book. He could never have got that idea of Mrs. Pipchin if he had attended to the text." A good example of the fidelity of the line drawing to the written word is provided by Browne's plate made to accompany the description of Mrs. Gamp's lodging in Chapter 49 of *Martin Chuzzlewit.*

practice, of course, owes much to fairy-tales and folk-lore which traditionally assume an animistic universe. The novelist frequently caricatures humorous eccentricities of appearance through their analogy with physical phenomena. Thus, for example, Gradgrind's drily positive manner is emphasized by his "hair, which bristled on the skirts of his bald head, a plantation of firs to keep the wind from its shining surface, all covered with knobs, like the crust of a plum pie, as if the head had scarcely warehouse-room for the hard facts stored inside." Conversely, more especially in the early writings, objects are endowed with human attributes. Gride's residence in *Nicholas Nickleby* is personified in the following terms:

In an old house, dismal dark and dusty, which seemed to have withered, like himself, and to have grown yellow and shrivelled in hoarding him from the light of day, as he had, in hoarding his money, lived Arthur Gride. Meagre old chairs and tables, of spare and bony make, and hard and cold as misers' hearts, were ranged in grim array against the gloomy walls; attenuated presses, grown lank and lantern-jawed in guarding the treasures they inclosed, and tottering, as though from constant fear and dread of thieves, shrunk up in dark corners, whence they cast no shadows on the ground, and seemed to hide and cower from observation. A tall grim clock upon the stairs, with long lean hands and famished face, ticked in cautious whispers; and when it struck the time, in thin and piping sounds like an old man's voice, it rattled, as if it were pinched with hunger.

No fireside couch was there, to invite repose and comfort. Elbow-chairs there were, but they looked uneasy in their minds, cocked their arms suspiciously and timidly, and kept on their guard. Others, were fantastically grim and gaunt, as having drawn themselves up to their utmost height, and put on their fiercest looks to stare all comers out of countenance. Others, again, knocked up against their neighbours, or leaned for support against the wall— somewhat ostentatiously, as if to call all men to witness that they were not worth the taking. The dark square lumbering bedsteads seemed built for restless dreams. The musty hangings seemed to creep in scanty folds together, whispering among themselves, when rustled by the wind, their trembling knowledge of the tempting wares that lurked within the dark and tight-locked closets.

As the recurrent phrases "as if," "as though," "seemed," "looked," "like" testify, there is here no pretense of literal realism; rather the yoking of discrepant images so associates the old miser with his possessions that they mirror his character and way of life.

In the novels of his maturity Dickens tended to abandon the use of animistic detail for a more poetic handling of the pathetic fallacy. Increasingly, the natural world is pictured as embodying principles of moral order which do not so much reflect as stand in judgment on human activities. In the remarkable description of the landscape through which he passes on his way to murder Tigg, Jonas Chuzzlewit is subjected to the mute but unwavering scrutiny of trees, likened to "sentinels of God":

The fishes slumbered in the cold, bright, glistening streams and rivers, perhaps; and the birds roosted on the branches of the trees; and in their stalls and pastures beasts were quiet; and human creatures slept. But what of that, when the solemn night was watching, when it never winked, when its darkness watched no less than its light! The stately trees, the moon and shining stars, the softly-stirring wind, the over-shadowed lane, the broad, bright country-side, they all kept watch. There was not a blade of growing grass or corn, but watched; and the quieter it was, the more intent and fixed its watch upon him seemed to be.

The glow of the evening sky takes on a symbolic hue, as Riderhood watches Bradley Headstone stalk Eugene Wrayburn:

The boat went on, under the arching trees, and over their tranquil shadows in the water. The bargeman, skulking on the opposite bank of the stream, went on after it. Sparkles of light showed Riderhood when and where the rower dipped his blades, until, even as he stood idly watching, the sun went down and the landscape was dyed red. And then the red had the appearance of fading out of it and mounting up to Heaven, as we say that blood, guiltily shed, does.

Significant in the present connection are the violent storms which so often herald climactic events in the later novels. Like the tempests in *Julius Caesar*, *Macbeth*, and *King Lear*, which also portend retribution, these seem to express nature's revulsion at man's inhumanity. The full scope of the novelist's pictorial imagination is elicited in the intensely dramatic rendering of the natural disturbances which are the prelude to Steerforth's drowning, Magwitch's return, and the murderous deeds of Bradley Headstone and John Jasper. In contrast, nature, represented in her most benign aspect, irradiates the settings for the pathetic deaths of such characters as Smike, Nell, Paul Dombey, Stephen Blackpool, and Betty Higden.

Whether the characters be virtuous or evil, their deaths are always for Dickens a solemn matter, and he sets the stage with corresponding care.* As has been earlier pointed out, although the villains of the

* The novelist's style unfailingly rises to a tone of exaltation in describing the moment of death, as if to suggest that all beings are equally dignified in its presence. In *Hard Times*, for example, Dickens provides for those two bewildered victims of life's muddle, Mrs. Gradgrind and Stephen Blackpool, an equivalent release. Of the former's passing he writes: ". . . Mrs. Gradgrind, emerged from the shadow in which man walketh and disquieteth himself in vain, took upon her the dread solemnity of the sages and patriarchs." And of Stephen at the end: "The star had shown him where to find the God of the poor; and through humility, and sorrow, and forgiveness, he had gone to his Redeemer's rest."

stories more often than not die by apparent accident, the natural forces which destroy them appear as the instruments of an avenging destiny. A number of such deaths occur by water. Quilp's drowning, while the knocking at the gate he has barred sounds in his ears, is a fittingly sardonic close to his cruel career. Of his body, flung by the tide on a swamp where pirates were once gibbeted, Dickens writes:

And there it lay, alone. The sky was red with flame, and the water that bore it there had been tinged with the sullen light as it flowed along. The place the deserted carcase had left so recently, a living man, was now a blazing ruin. There was something of the glare upon its face. The hair, stirred by the damp breeze, played in a kind of mockery of death—such mockery as the dead man himself would have delighted in when alive—about its head, and its dress fluttered idly in the night wind.

Both Gaffer Hexam and Rogue Riderhood are drawn down into the river from which they derived their ghoulish livelihood, and the same end lies in store for Steerforth, Compeyson, and Bradley Headstone. Although the means are different, the violent deaths of Carker and Blandois come on them with like inevitability; the locomotive which tears the one to pieces and the house which crushes the other seem by foreordination only to have been awaiting the appointed time.

The opening scenes of many of Dickens' mature novels present different but no less conclusive evidence of his mastery over the uses to which setting can be put. All of the works prior to *Dombey and Son* begin on a tentative and irresolute note, indicative of the author's uncertainty about what was to come. The leisurely start of *Nicholas Nickleby* is typical in its irrelevance:

There once lived, in a sequestered part of the county of Devonshire, one Mr. Godfrey Nickleby: a worthy gentleman, who, taking it into his head rather late in life that he must get married, and not being young enough or rich enough to aspire to the hand of a lady of fortune, had wedded an old flame out of mere attachment, who in her turn had taken him for the same reason. Thus two people who cannot afford to play cards for money, sometimes sit down to a quiet game for love.

In contrast, *Dombey and Son* plunges *in medias res*; the introductory description not only leads straight into the story, but ironically forecasts its principal thematic concern:

Dombey sat in the corner of the darkened room in the great arm-chair by the bedside, and Son lay tucked up warm in a little basket bedstead, carefully disposed on a low settee immediately in front of the fire and close to it, as if his constitution were analogous to that of a muffin, and it was essential to toast him brown while he was very new.

The exigencies of space in the shorter novels written for weekly serialization required that the writer exercise the strictest economy in getting his initial effects. A good example is the description of the schoolroom which is the setting for Gradgrind's inquisition at the beginning of *Hard Times*:

The square finger, moving here and there, lighted suddenly on Bitzer, perhaps because he chanced to sit in the same ray of sunlight which, darting in at one of the bare windows of the intensely whitewashed room, irradiated Sissy. For, the boys and girls sat on the face of the inclined plane in two compact bodies, divided up the centre by a narrow interval; and Sissy, being at the corner of a row on the sunny side, came in for the beginning of a sunbeam, of which Bitzer, being at the corner of a row on the other side, a few rows in advance, caught the end.

But, whereas the girl was so dark-eyed and dark-haired, that she seemed to receive a deeper and more lustrous colour from the sun, when it shone upon her, the boy was so light-eyed and light-haired that the self-same rays appeared to draw out of him what little colour he ever possessed. His cold eyes would hardly have been eyes, but for the short ends of lashes which, by bringing them into immediate contrast with something paler than themselves, expressed their form. His short-cropped hair might have been a mere continuation of the sandy freckles on his forehead and face. His skin was so unwholesomely deficient in the natural tinge, that he looked as though, if he were cut, he would bleed white.

The contents of this paragraph are conveyed exclusively in visual terms. The eye, following the sunray, perceives what it sequentially discloses. The distinguishing characteristics of Sissy and Bitzer are clearly established by their appearances; and the surface contrast thus brought out prepares for the conflict between the opposing wisdoms of the heart and head which will shape the ensuing action. In both *A Tale of Two Cities* and *Great Expectations* the narrative focus is similarly restricted at the outset to a single point of view, responsive to the pictorial aspects of the enveloping situation. In the former novel the reader nervously travels by the night mail to Dover in company with a mysterious passenger, who remains nameless for several pages; and in *Great Expectations* he shares Pip's uncomprehending terror at encountering Magwitch on the marshes.

Dickens' continuing preference for the full-scale novel in twenty monthly parts was prompted by the ampler scope it allowed for his descriptive talents, as well as for the multiplication of episodes and characters. In addition to supplying a suitably full context for the action, setting in the later novels is increasingly invested with thematic connotations. The introductory chapters of *Bleak House* and *Little Dorrit*, one evoking a foggy November day in London, the other a blazing August day in Marseilles, concentrate on the atmospheric properties of the *mis-en-scène*. Like a camera lens, the author's vision begins by "panning" with impersonal curiosity over a wide prospect, registering in rapid succession a selection of apparently random and discrete "shots" which gradually coalesce into coherent patterns. In the following passage from *Bleak House* the abrupt juxtaposition of prepositional, participial, and adverbial phrases in place of normal syntactic sentences contributes to the montage effect:

Fog everywhere. Fog up the river, where it flows among green aits and meadows; fog down the river, where it rolls defiled among the tiers of shipping, and the waterside pollutions of a great (and dirty) city. Fog on the Essex marshes, fog on the Kentish heights. Fog creeping into the cabooses of collier-brigs, fog lying out on the yards, and hovering in the rigging of great ships; fog drooping on the gunwales of barges and small boats. Fog in the eyes and throats of ancient Greenwich pensioners, wheezing by the firesides of their wards; fog in the stem and bowl of the afternoon pipe of the wrathful skipper, down in his close cabin; fog cruelly pinching the toes and fingers of his shivering little 'prentice boy on deck. Chance people on the bridges peeping over the parapets into a nether sky of fog, with fog all round them, as if they were up in a balloon, and hanging in the misty clouds.

The mode of access is penetrative. Attention is drawn steadily inward, converging and finally coming to rest on a central scene to which all of the antecedent impressions have been leading up. And this scene, the High Court of Chancery in *Bleak House*, the dungeon in *Little Dorrit*, not only provides the point of departure for the story but also defines its mood or tone.

Consistent with their beginnings, both *Bleak House* and *Little Dorrit* are spatially organized primarily in terms of settings, although in the first novel these are presented extensively, and in the second intensively. The homogeneity of the social world in *Bleak House* is to a large extent conveyed by the interdependence of the localities which define its boundaries. Thus, the transition from the Court of Chancery in the first chapter to Chesney Wold in the second is achieved through this paragraph:

It is but a glimpse of the world of fashion that we want on this same miry afternoon. It is not so unlike the Court of Chancery, but that we may pass from one scene to the other, as the crow flies. Both the world of fashion and the Court of Chancery are things of precedent and usage; oversleeping Rip Van Winkles, who have played at strange games through a deal of thundery weather; sleeping beauties, whom the Knight will wake one day, when all the stopped spits in the kitchen shall begin to turn prodigiously!

In Chapter 5 the locale shifts to Krook's Rag and Bottle Warehouse, adjacent to the Court of Chancery and mockingly called by the same name, as another repository of litter and outmoded rubbish. And Chapters 11 and 16 describe the noisome slum Tom-all-Alone's which is the physical counterpart of the moral contamination stemming from the case of Jarndyce and Jarndyce. "What connexion," asks the author,

can there be, between the place in Lincolnshire, the house in town, the Mercury in powder, and the whereabouts of Jo the outlaw with the broom, who had that distant ray of light upon him when he swept the churchyard step? What connexion can there have been between many people in the innumerable histories of this world, who, from opposite sides of great gulfs, have nevertheless, been very curiously brought together!

It is not true, as is often stated, that the fog associated with the obscurantism of the law court in the opening of *Bleak House* metaphorically embraces the entire novel. Each setting has its analogous atmosphere; rain at Chesney Wold, soot in Krook's establishment, dust in the law chambers of Tulkinghorn and Vholes. More pervasive than all is the pestilence that emanates from the burial ground where Captain Hawdon lies and of which Jo is the emissary. Of this personified plague spot, festering at the heart of the novel, Dickens writes:

But he has his revenge. Even the winds are his messengers, and they serve him in these hours of darkness. There is not a drop of Tom's corrupted blood but propagates infection and contagion everywhere. It shall pollute, this very night, the choice stream (in which chemists on analysis would find the genuine nobility) of a Norman house, and his Grace shall not be able say Nay to the infamous alliance. There is not an atom of Tom's slime, not a cubic inch of any pestilential gas in which he lives, not one obscenity or degradation about him, not an ignorance, not a wickedness, not a brutality of his committing, but shall work its retribution, through every order of society, up to the proudest of the proud, and to the highest of the high. Verily, what with tainting, plundering, and spoiling, Tom has his revenge.

In *Little Dorrit*, as in *Bleak House*, the settings are so arranged as to interlock the strands of the narrative. In the later novel, however, the author's moral indignation more insistently goes beyond social evils to excoriate the stupidity of mind and the hardness of heart which are their breeding ground; and as a result the physical circumstances of environment are more closely identified with their spiritual effects. *Little Dorrit* is a novel of imprisoning interiors. The gaol at Marseilles where the story commences is structurally balanced by the Grande Chartreuse in which the characters are assembled at the beginning of the second book. The impression that society is made up of institutions which hold their inmates in bondage, whether forced or voluntary, is cumulatively intensified by one setting after another: the quarantine station, the Marshalsea, the Circumlocution Office, Bleeding Heart Yard, even "that dreary red-brick dungeon at Hampton Court" where Mrs. Gowan resides. But individuals are not less hermetically sealed off in their private prisons; for in this book even those who are nominally at liberty have out of covert guilt passed sentence on themselves. Mrs. Clennam, shut up in a falling house, thinks of herself as "in prison, and in bonds. . . ." Arthur, visiting Casby's residence, steps into a "sober, silent, air-tight house—one might have fancied it to have been stifled by Mutes in the Eastern manner—and the door, closing again, seemed to shut out sound and motion." There are as well Merdle's gloomy mansion, where the parrot screeches derisively from his golden cage; the dreary hiding places in which Miss Wade secretes herself and Tattycoram; the tomblike palaces which William Dorrit rents in Venice and Rome. Of his heroine's response to her existence in Italy, Dickens writes:

It appeared on the whole, to Little Dorrit herself, that this same society in which they lived, greatly resembled a superior sort of Marshalsea. Numbers of people seemed to come abroad, pretty much as people had come into the prison; through debt, through idleness, relationship, curiosity, and general unfitness for getting on at home. . . . They had precisely the same incapacity for settling down to anything, as the prisoners used to have; they rather deteriorated one another, as the prisoners used to do; and they wore untidy dresses, and fell into a slouching way of life: still, always like the people in the Marshalsea.

On his first arrival in London at the beginnings of Chapter 3, Arthur is greeted by the pall of gloom which lies over the city on Sundays:

It was a Sunday evening in London, gloomy, close and stale. Maddening church bells of all degrees of dissonance, sharp and flat, cracked and clear, fast and slow, made the brick-and-mortar echoes hideous. Melancholy streets in a penitential garb of soot, steeped the souls of the people who were condemned to look at them out of windows, in dire despondency. In every thoroughfare, up almost every alley, and down almost every turning, some doleful bell was throbbing, jerking, tolling, as if the Plague were in the city and the dead-carts were going round. Everything was bolted and barred that could by possibility furnish relief to an overworked people. No pictures, no unfamiliar animals, no rare plants or flowers, no natural or artificial wonders of the ancient world—all *taboo* with that enlightened strictness that the ugly South Sea gods in the British Museum might have supposed themselves at home again. Nothing to see but streets, streets, streets. Nothing to breathe but streets, streets, streets. Nothing to change the brooding mind, or raise it up. Nothing for the spent toiler to do, but to compare the monotony of his seventh day with the monotony of his six days, think what a weary life he led, and make the best of it—or the worst, according to the probabilities.

The desolating perspective thus implanted widens until it ultimately encompasses all humanity. For Clennam, self-incarcerated in the Marshalsea, comes to think his condition emblematic of the human lot, so that to his watching eyes the rays of the sun rising over London appear to be "bars of the prison of this lower world." And, as has been suggested, it is into a world so conceived that he and Amy, emancipated only because of their love for each other, step forth at the end of the novel.

In *Our Mutual Friend* each of the parallel plots

is initially identified with a specific setting, appropriate to its development. The first chapter is set on the Thames, whose waters will eventually wash away the barrier in rank between Eugene and Lizzie. The second chapter, describing the Veneerings' dinner party, introduces through discussion of old Harmon's legacy the different kind of social distinction based on material wealth which Rokesmith and Bella must surmount. At a deeper level of significance, however, the river and the dust-mounds polarize values whose interplay sets up a field of symbolic action. The two are equated by their common elements of filth, the detritus of a sordidly defiled society. Both incorporate decay and death; but the flowing waters, in contrast to the inert mass of the mounds, also hold forth the possibility of spiritual rebirth, like the Thames in Eliot's *The Waste Land*. Riderhood, "baptized unto death," comes back from immersion unregenerate and so is doomed to death by drowning, as are Gaffer Hexam and Bradley Headstone. On the other hand, Rokesmith and Eugene find the river life-giving, and dying unto themselves, are reborn with cleansed hearts and spirits redirected to the good of others.

Dickens, however, never allows the symbolic overtones adducible from the settings of his later novels to obscure their literal immediacy in furthering the narrative, illuminating character, or focusing social criticism. Tom-all-Alone's tangibly exhales an atmosphere of corruption; William Dorrit is visibly marked with the taint of the Marshalsea; and the Thames in its windings through *Our Mutual Friend* links many of the pivotal events in the novel. A memorandum for the first number states: "Open between the bridges"; and the opening riverscape precisely locates the place "between Southwark Bridge which is of iron, and London Bridge which is of stone."

Dickens' continuing exploration of his artistic resources in *The Mystery of Edwin Drood* is immediately evident in the extraordinary handling of the novel's introductory scene. Setting is evoked entirely through the drugged perceptions of John Jasper, as he lies in an opium den in the London dock area:

An ancient English Cathedral Tower? How can the ancient English Cathedral Tower be here! The well-known massive gray square tower of its old Cathedral? How can that be here! There is no spike of rusty iron in the air, between the eye and it, from any point of the real prospect. What is the spike that intervenes, and who has set it up? Maybe it is set up by the Sultan's orders for the impaling of a horde of Turkish robbers, one by one. It is so, for cymbals clash, and the Sultan goes by to his palace in long procession. Ten thousand scimitars flash in the sunlight, and thrice ten thousand dancing-girls strew flowers. Then, follow white elephants caparisoned in countless gorgeous colours, and infinite in number and attendants. Still the Cathedral Tower rises in the background, where it cannot be, and still no writhing figure is on the grim spike. Stay! Is the spike so low a thing as the rusty spike on the top of a post of an old bedstead that has tumbled all awry? Some vague period of drowsy laughter must be devoted to the consideration of this possibility.

Even in its truncated state, this last story progressed far enough to expand many of the hints which lurk in the foregoing paragraph. The chaotic impressions streaming through Jasper's mind mingle in inextricable confusion the two worlds which he inhabits, the nether depths of London and the cathedral city of Cloisterham, also mined with corruption under its decorous surface; while the crazy visions of Oriental revelry which bedazzle his senses seem, in addition, to foreshadow the exotic eastern strain so mysteriously woven throughout the texture of the existing narrative.

These settings are not only correlative with the opposing sides of Jasper's dual nature; they also determine his actions and provide almost all the available clues for resolving the mystery. Dickens claimed that he had "a very curious and new idea for my new story"; and Forster wrote that its originality "was to consist in the review of the murderer's career by himself at the close, when its temptations were to be dwelt upon as if, not he the culprit, but some other man, were the tempted. The last chapters were to be written in the condemned cell, to which his wickedness, all elaborately elicited from him as if told of another, had brought him." Both assertions are substantiated by the technique of the novel's opening scene, which graphically projects the *paysage intérieur* of schizophrenia. Setting could yield no richer harvest of implication.

Chronology of Novels

The novels of Charles Dickens were first published at the dates and in the form indicated below:

Pickwick Papers Monthly numbers, April 1836 to November 1837

Oliver Twist Monthly serial in *Bentley's Miscellany*, February 1837 to April 1839 (24 installments)

Nicholas Nickleby Monthly numbers, April 1838 to October 1839

The Old Curiosity Shop Weekly serial in *Master Humphrey's Clock*, April 25, 1840, to February 6, 1841

Barnaby Rudge Weekly serial in *Master Humphrey's Clock*, February 13, 1841, to November 27, 1841

Martin Chuzzlewit Monthly numbers, January 1843 to July 1844

Dombey and Son Monthly numbers, October 1846 to April 1848

David Copperfield Monthly numbers, May 1849 to November 1850

Bleak House Monthly numbers, March 1852 to September 1853

Hard Times Weekly serial in *Household Words*, April 1, 1854, to August 12, 1854

Little Dorrit Monthly numbers, December 1855 to June 1857

A Tale of Two Cities Weekly serial in *All the Year Round*, April 30, 1859, to November 26, 1859

Great Expectations Weekly serial in *All the Year Round*,
December 1, 1860 to August 3, 1861

Our Mutual Friend Monthly numbers, May 1864 to November 1865

The Mystery of Edwin Drood Monthly numbers, April
1870 to September 1870 (six of twelve numbers completed)

Bibliographical Note

All passages from Dickens' novels cited in the foregoing pages have been taken from the Gadshill Edition, *38 vols. (1897–1908). The most readily accessible complete edition is* The New Oxford Illustrated Dickens, *21 vols. (1947–1958). The long-standing need for a critical edition of the novelist's work is now being met by* The Clarendon Edition, *the first volume of which,* Oliver Twist, *edited by Kathleen Tillotson, appeared in 1966. Other editions of single novels which include textual commentary are:* Hard Times, *edited by George H. Ford and Sylvère Monod and* Great Expectations, *edited by Edgar Rosenberg, both in* The Norton Critical Editions; *and* David Copperfield, *edited by George H. Ford in Riverside Editions.*

The three most important collections of Dickens' correspondence are: the Nonesuch Press Letters of Charles Dickens, *3 vols. (1938), edited by Walter Dexter; Mr. and Mrs. Charles Dickens: His Letters to Her (1935), edited by Walter Dexter; and* The Heart of Charles Dickens, *As Revealed in His Letters to Angela Burdett-Coutts (1952), edited by Edgar Johnson. All of the foregoing will be superseded, however, by the magnificent Pilgrim Edition of* The Letters of Charles Dickens, *the first volume of which, edited by Madeline House and Graham Storey, was published in 1965.*

Another important primary source is The Speeches of Charles Dickens *(1960), edited by K. J. Fielding.*

The two essential biographies of the novelist are John Forster's The Life of Charles Dickens, *which should be read in the edition edited by J. W. T. Ley (1928); and Edgar Johnson's* Charles Dickens: His Tragedy and Triumph, *2 vols. (1952).*

For the historical context of Dickens' writings, the following may be especially recommended: Humphry House, The Dickens World *(1941); and two studies by Philip Collins,* Dickens and Crime *(1962) and* Dickens and Education *(1963).*

The best accounts of Dickens' writing habits are contained in Dickens Romancier: Étude sur la création littéraire dans les romans de Charles Dickens *(1953) by Sylvère Monod;* and in* Dickens at Work *(1957) by John Butt and Kathleen Tillotson. George H. Ford in* Dickens and His Readers: Aspects of Novel-Criticism since 1836 *(1955) exhaustively surveys the novelist's literary reputation.*

Three classics of Dickens criticism continue to hold their ground: Charles Dickens: A Critical Study *(1898) and* Critical Studies of the Works of Charles Dickens *(1924), both by George Gissing; and* Charles Dickens: A Critical Study *(1906) by G. K. Chesterton. Among more recent critical studies, two are outstanding: J. Hillis Miller,* Charles Dickens: The World of His Novels *(1959); and Steven Marcus,* Dickens from Pickwick to Dombey *(1965). Much of the best writing about Dickens has appeared in the form of articles. Two recent collections contain a generous sampling of varying critical approaches to the novelist:* The Dickens Critics *(1961), edited by George H. Ford and Lauriat Lane, Jr., which covers the*

---

* Since the completion of the present volume Professor Monod has published an English version of his work, with substantial revisions (*Dickens the Novelist*, 1968).

period from the mid-nineteenth century to the present; and Dickens in the Twentieth Century (*1962*), *edited by John Gross and Gabriel Pearson.*

Readers who wish to carry farther their study of Dickens should consult the very full bibliographical essay by Ada Nisbit in Victorian Fiction: A Guide to Research (*1964*), *edited by Lionel Stevenson.*

Index